Awed to Heaven,
Rooted in Earth

Awed to Heaven, Rooted in Earth

Prayers of Walter Brueggemann

Edited by Edwin Searcy

FORTRESS PRESS / MINNEAPOLIS

AWED TO HEAVEN, ROOTED IN EARTH
PRAYERS OF WALTER BRUEGGEMANN

Cover photo: Kaz Mori / Getty Images. Used by permission.
Cover and book design: Zan Ceeley

Library of Congress Cataloging-in-Publication Data
Brueggemann, Walter.
    Awed to heaven, rooted in earth : prayers of Walter Brueggemann / edited
    by Edwin Searcy.
        p. cm.
    Includes index.
    ISBN 0-8006-3460-8 (pbk. : alk. paper)
    ISBN 0-8006-3610-4 (hardcover : alk. paper)
    1. Prayers. I. Searcy, Edwin. II. Title.
    BV245.B677 2003
    242'.8—dc21   2002153172

The paper used in this publication meets the minimum requirements of American National Standard for Information Sciences — Permanence of Paper for Printed Library Materials, ANSI Z329.48-1984.

Printed in Canada

07   06   05   04   03   3   4   5   6   7   8   9   10

For
a long stream of treasured faculty colleagues —
twenty-five years worth
at Eden Theological Seminary
and seventeen years worth
at Columbia Theological Seminary
with thanks and appreciation

3. Against your absence — A hidden God

4. We are ready to listen — For illumination

5. Move off the page — While reading texts

6. Awed to heaven, rooted in earth —
For the church in mission

7. Start again — For a bruised world

Editor's Foreword

The first thing a student in Walter Brueggemann's class notices are the prayers. Each class, each day begins with evocative prayer, crafted for the moment and offered with daring humility. This is not a rote exercise to be dispensed with lightly. In this disciplined practice, teacher becomes pastor, speaking for a classroom become congregation. In these prayers Brueggemann risks naming the truth about us, about the world, and about the God who is at once listening and speaking.

The care that Brueggemann gives to his prayers testifies to the crucial importance that he places on the living covenantal conversation. For him the biblical texts offer the mother tongue of the divine-human conversation. In his prayers for class and for worship, Brueggemann speaks this mother tongue of praise and confession, lament and gratitude, despair and faithfulness. Listening to his practiced voice we rediscover ancient ways of speaking honestly before God.

Brueggemann has written that "the preacher speaks in another language, a language not frontal but subtle, a voice not assaulting but surprising, speech not predictable but faithful in its daring. That other language of evangelical possibility is spoken with the gentle quiet of a dove, with the dread-filled cunning of a serpent."[1] Brueggemann's prayers are all of these things — subtle, surprising and daring, gentle and dread-filled. They echo the poetic speech of the psalms and of the prophets. They testify to Brueggemann's faith in the God of exodus and exile, cross and empty tomb. They offer hope to a church whose truth-telling voice has often been tamed and muted.

I am a pastor of one such church. The congregation that I serve lives the exilic existence that Brueggemann names as the location of the North American church. The sale of the congregation's building and property reflected the loss of its former identity as a neighborhood church. A small, aging remnant leased worship space and wondered what the future would hold. Now, fifteen years later, a vital congregation is growing in faithfulness and discipleship. At the heart of this missional energy is a recovery — in our preaching and praying — of the daring speech that is our biblical mother tongue. In all of this, Walter Brueggemann's living witness has given us courage to practice this truth-telling speech with one another and before God.

The privilege of editing this collection has included the opportunity to read the prayers with congregants and colleagues. I am grateful to this trusted group — Daphne and Terry Anderson, Doug Goodwin, Gerald Hobbs, Keith Howard, Elisabeth Jones, Janice and Jim Love, Anne and George Searcy — for their shared wisdom. In particular, Janice Love's careful reading of the prayers, suggestion for this volume's title, and assistance in compiling the biblical index has been a great gift.

Finally, with scores of other students, I am immensely grateful that I call Walter Brueggemann teacher, friend, and pastor.

EDWIN SEARCY
UNIVERSITY HILL CONGREGATION
VANCOUVER, CANADA

Note

1. Walter Brueggemann, *Finally Comes the Poet: Daring Speech for Proclamation* (Minneapolis: Fortress Press, 1989), 141–42.

Preface

It is a long-standing practice to open seminary classes with prayer, a practice well-honored in the lectures of John Calvin. The substantive intention of such prayer is to invoke God's guidance and the teaching presence of the spirit, acknowledging that the learning now to transpire is not any ordinary learning such as the transformation of information, but rather it is an exercise in faith, obedience, and praise. That is, "loving God with one's mind." That awesome task and privilege cannot be rightly done apart from God's presence and guidance. Alongside that substantive act of submission and petition, prayer at the opening of class is a heavily symbol-laden act, for it situates knowledge in the context of faith. It articulates a proper ratio of reason to faith and quite practically asserts that learning takes place with a cloud of witnesses who have believed and trusted before the present company and who believe and trust presently alongside the immediate body of teachers and learners. Thus prayer at the beginning of class in a seminary is not a mere convention — though it is that. It is an act of rightly framing the instruction of the day among a body of believers or would-be believers who are unafraid of the task of learning.

These prayers are among those that I have offered in class over a long ministry of teaching. Obviously they do not include all of them because many were extemporaneous and soon forgotten — at least on the human side of the praying endeavor. Over time I have come to think that such prayers require great intentionality in order to situate in prayer the learning agenda of the day, to locate teacher and students in the ongoing life of the church in whose service we learn, and to ponder the condition of the world that is the proper though sometimes disregarded context of all evangelical learning. Over time, of course, my sense of proper prayer in the context of instruction has evolved, changed, and I hope grown. I have come to think (1) that because so much seminary prayer is routinized repetition that such prayers need to be "figured" in fresh ways, and (2) that the field of imagination for such "figuring" is scripture. As a result my prayers offered in class have increasingly become prayers "back to scripture" — a practice I learned alongside my friend David Grant, a practice more readily undertaken by a scripture teacher than colleagues in other disciplines.

Offering and leading such prayers is one thing — it is an attempt to gather the energies and imaginations of students into a shared act of faithful focus for a brief period of time. To reproduce such prayers in a published form is a quite different matter and requires at least a modest justification. I can think of two such justifications. First, I have come to think that much public prayer in the church is careless and slovenly, and that what passes for spontaneity is in fact lack of preparation. Thus, I believe that public prayers must be "well-said" in an artful way, not to call attention to the artistry itself but to mobilize and sustain the attention of the praying community. Such prayer must be artful enough to be porous, in order to allow the words uttered to be access points for other members of the praying assembly who may take these utterances as their utterances, a point I have learned from my friend Thomas Green. Green writes:

> What makes public speech public? My hunch is that *public speech occurs when what is said in one person's speech is heard by others as candidates for their own speech.*[1]

I understand that prayers in the seminary classroom cannot be easily transposed into a more proper church setting, but I believe that these prayers may be suggestive resources for those who habitually utter public prayer. I believe that in an intensely secularized context the task of prayer is to re-imagine our life in the presence of God and therefore offer direct address to God — that playfully said invites interaction with the God who has pledged to hear. I have intended these prayers to be modestly venturesome, not to call attention to the prayers themselves but because prayer is characteristically a dangerous act, and dangerous rhetoric is required to match the intent of the act. It is an awesome matter to voice one's life before God, and our lives should therefore be awesomely uttered. One need not seek very carefully to find in these prayers the conventional concerns of praise, confession, petition, and intercession. I have come to think, however, that such recurring evangelical accents should not be uttered in the fashion of a grocery list but uttered with the freshness of obedient evangelical rhetoric. So, first, I hope that these prayers will aid others in the act of public prayer.

Second, this collection of prayers may be justified as an act of gratitude. These prayers are published in my last semester of teaching after forty-one years of teaching and praying. Over that time I have of course studied with a variegated assemblage of students. For some of them I have been a treasured teacher, for others not at all. But all of them, by choice or not, prayed with me, and some I have found to be more mature in prayer than I. Thus, as I move toward retirement this book of prayers is an acknowledgment of and thanks to those students, because every reflective teacher knows that quality teaching is largely evoked by quality students. And as I thank students so I acknowledge a host of teaching colleagues at Eden Theological Seminary and Columbia Theological Seminary who have taught and prayed alongside me in a company of friendship, trust, and conflict over these years. My appreciation for and thanks to such colleagues is beyond measure.

The completion of this manuscript evokes thanks toward many quarters. Jack Gergen, my student of long ago and now deceased, made the initial collection of my class prayers, which he recorded and then offered in an informal publication that led to my thought about gathering them together. Tia Foley has done a great deal of work readying the manuscript, completing the efforts of Tempie Alexander. Tim Simpson has as usual worked to make the manuscript workable. The folks at Fortress Press have been characteristically helpful and my thanks to K. C. Hanson is deep and wide. Most of all I am grateful to Ed Searcy, who has worked long and well over these prayers, making judgments, ordering, cataloguing, and sorting, but most of all praying these prayers in the context of a local congregation. That he has been aided by members of his congregation in Vancouver, Canada, nicely articulates the linkage between a praying seminary classroom and a praying congregation that has mattered to me during all of these years of teaching ministry.

I will have other occasions to reflect on forty-one years of teaching as I retire, but no occasion is more freighted for me than this one in which to ponder my happy circumstance in two seminaries where I have taught, learned, and prayed all this time. If it were not ostentatious to do so, this long season would culminate in a glad, grateful Nunc Dimittis. The church at prayer is the only adequate matrix for theological education and so, after many thanks to my colleagues, the proper way to finish is in praise and thanksgiving.

WALTER BRUEGGEMANN
COLUMBIA THEOLOGICAL SEMINARY

Note

1. Thomas F. Greene, *Voices: The Educational Formation of Conscience* (Notre Dame, Ind.: University of Notre Dame Press, 1999), 156.

1

And then you — Facing God

And then you

We arrange our lives as best we can,
 to keep your holiness at bay,
  with our pieties,
   our doctrines,
   our liturgies,
   our moralities,
   our secret ideologies,
Safe, virtuous, settled.
And then you —
 you and your dreams,
 you and your visions,
 you and your purposes,
 you and your commands,
 you and our neighbors.
We find your holiness not at bay,
 but probing, pervading,
  insisting, demanding.
And we yield, sometimes gladly,
 sometimes resentfully,
 sometimes late . . . or soon.
We yield because you, beyond us, are our God.
 We are your creatures met by your holiness,
  by your holiness made our true selves.
 And we yield. Amen.

Old Testament theology / October 15, 1998

At the dawn

Our first glimpse of reality this day — everyday — is your fidelity.
We are dazzled by the ways you remain constant among us,
      in season, out of season,
      for better, for worse,
      in sickness and in health.
You are there in watchfulness as we fall asleep;
You are there in alertness when we awaken . . . and we are glad.
    Before the day ends, we will have occasion
        to flag your absence in indifference . . .
        but not now, not at the dawn.
    Before the day ends, we will think more than once
        that we need a better deal from you . . .
        but not now, not at the dawn.
    Before the day ends, we will look away from you and
        relish our own fidelity and our virtue in mercy . . .
        but not now, not at the dawn.
Now, at the dawn, our eyes are fixed on you in gladness.
    We ask only that your faithfulness
        permeate every troubled place we are able to name,
        that your mercy
        move against the hurts to make new,
        that your steadfastness
        hold firmly what is too fragile on its own.
And we begin the day in joy, in hope, and in deep gladness. Amen.

Old Testament theology class, on God's defining adjectives / July 18, 2000

You live at the hinge

You brood in the night in its fearfulness,
You dawn the day in its energy,
     You move at the edge of night
        into the margin of day.
     You live at the hinge between fear and energy.
You take the feeble night and give us strong day,
     You take our fatigue and bestow courage,
     You take our drowsy reluctance and fashion full-blooded zeal.
What shall we say?
     You, only you, you
     You at the hinge — and then the day.
You — and then us,
     from you in faithfulness,
     us for the day,
     us in the freedom and courage and energy,
     and then back to you — in trust and gratitude.
Amen.

Allegheny College / August 17, 1989

Stunned by the morning

The night of defeat is long and still and unbearable.
We know the nights.
And our sisters and brothers
    who are cold,
    and hungry,
    and brutalized know them better than do we.
And you also know the night in Ashdod and in a trillion other times.
How it is with you in the night we do not know.
Perhaps it is like it is with us.
We, with the Philistines, are stunned by the morning.
            stunned to find our pet projects toppled.
            stunned to find our favorite gods failed.
            stunned to find our managed hopes defeated.
Then you in the morning.
You only.
You in splendor.
You in glory.
You in power.
This day we dazzle at your glory in the midst of our long night.
Move in your glory this day in the midst of our many nights.
Bring us to your day.
To your new day.
Your third day. Amen.

On Reading 1 Samuel 5 / March 2, 2000

We wait for you to ache

With the energy we have,
    we begin the day,
    waiting and watching and hoping.

We wait,
    not clear about our waiting.
But filled with a restlessness,
    daring to imagine
    that you are not finished yet —
    so we wait,
    patiently, impatiently,
    restlessly, confidently,
    quaking and fearful,
    boldly and daring.

Your sovereign decree stands clear
    and we do not doubt.
We wait for you to dissolve in tender tears.
Your impervious rule takes no prisoners,
    we wait for you to ache and hurt and care over us
    and with us
    and beyond us.
        Cry with us the brutality
        grieve with us the misery
        tremble with us the poverty and hurt.
Attend to us — by attending in power and in mercy,
    remake this alien world into our proper home.

We pray in the name of the utterly homeless one,
    even Jesus.

Amen.

Alleghany College / August 16, 1989

You . . . and therefore us

The day demands that we begin in praise of you,
    for the day is yours and we are yours;
    we could not live the day without reference to you,
            without your gifts,
            without your commands.
We begin with praise,
    for the gift of life,
    for the gift of our life together,
    for the gift of life in your world
        with all your beloved creatures,
    for the gift of life in your church
        with your steady recital of wonders.
You, you alone, only you,
    you who made and makes and remakes heaven and earth,
    you who executes justice and gives food we know not how,
    you who sets prisoners free and sights the blind,
    you who lifts up and watches and upholds,
    you who reigns forever,
    you . . . and therefore us.
You, except we turn to lesser trusts,
    all of us with our trust in the powers,
You, except we turn to ignoble aims,
    all of us preoccupied with ourselves.
You, except we invest in our little controls and our larger fears,
    all of us marked by anxiety.
And then we watch as you ease us out of anxiety,
        as you heal our selves turned new,
        as you topple powers and bring new chances
            for truthful public life.
You . . . except . . . but then finally, always, everywhere you . . .
        and us on the receiving end.
And we are grateful. Amen.

On reading Psalm 146, the day Milosovich fell in Belgrade,
Campbell Seminar / October 16, 2000

A thousand, a million, a trillion tongues

O for a thousand tongues to sing
    our great redeemer's name;
To sing beyond ourselves, extravagantly,
            with abandonment,
          beyond all our possibilities,
            and all our fears,
            and all our hopes . . .
to our redeemer dear, the antidote to our death,
        the salve to our wounds,
        the resolve of our destructiveness . . .
A thousand, a million, a trillion tongues,
        more than our own,
        more than our tradition,
        more than our theology,
        more than our understanding,
     tongues around us,
     tongues among us,
     tongues from our silenced parts.
Tongues from us to you in freedom and in courage,
Finally ceding our lives and our loves to your good care. Amen.

Old Testament Introduction, for O'Connor and Yoder on Psalms /
November 20, 1998

For how you hope

God sovereign and generous,
>who commands the rise and fall of the nations,
>who calls and has chosen many peoples,
>who weeps when they harm each other,
>who haunts every local culture — including ours —
>>with your will for well-being,
>who draws close to the powerless and
>>surprises with power via weakness . . .

You are the one whom we praise in astonishment,
>>we adore in gladness,
>>we thank in gratitude . . .

>for who you are,
>for what you do,
>for how you hope.

Look with mercy on us this day,
>>on all the churches we serve and love,
>>on all the people we name,
>>on all the communities so fragile in which
>>we are embedded.

Look with your mercy, and we will obey you all the day long.
>In the name of Jesus who obeyed fully. Amen.

On reading Isaiah 19:23-25, lecture by Thomas Thangaraj / October 11, 2000

We say "Yes, yes"

Holy God, to whom we turn in our trouble,
    and from whom we receive life and well-being
        even in the face of death;
Here we are now in the great congregation.
    We come here to bear witness of you to our brothers and sisters;
    We come here to bear witness because we cannot do otherwise;
    We come here to hear the witness of our sisters and brothers,
        without whose witness we cannot live.
We gladly and without reservation assert:
    You are the one who gives life;
    You are the one who hears our prayers;
    You are the one who turns our jungles of threat
        into peaceable zones of life;
    You are the one who has kept us since birth,
        who stands by us in our failure and shame;
        who moves against our anxiety to make us free.
    You are the one who does not hide your face when we call.
So we praise you.   We worship you.   We adore you.
    We yield our life over to you in glad thanksgiving.
    As an act of praise, we submit our sick and our dead to you;
    As an act of praise, we submit more and more
        of our own life to you;
    As an act of praise we notice your poor,
        and pledge our energy on their behalf;
    As an act of praise we say "yes" to you and to your rule over us.
    We say "yes, yes,"
    Amen and Amen.

Psalm 22:21b-31 / January 13, 1997

You with ears bent close to our lips

You, you are the one we address,
    always you,
        only you . . .   who has given us life,
                    who waits for us to answer.
We, toward you, speak and remain tongue-tied,
    for we lack words that are honest enough,
                and dangerous enough,
                and fierce enough to match you.
We do not speak first, but after our mothers and fathers,
    who knew cadences of honesty about our troubles,
    who knew cadences of danger about your presence,
    who knew cadences of fierceness to fit our rage and loss.
So we speak to you words that we have always spoken:
    words of praise and adoration:
        . . . into your gates with thanksgiving,
        into your courts with praise . . .
    words of confession and remorse:
        . . . against you and only you have we sinned . . .
    words of thanks and astonishment:
        . . . you have turned our mourning into dancing . . .
    words of rage unabated:
        . . . dash their heads against the rocks.
So many words we need to speak
    to you from whom no secret can be hid,
    you beyond us, you with us, you for us,
    you with ears bent close to our lips,
You . . . and our woes turned toward you, always you, only you,
    yet again you.
Amen.

Approaching the Psalter / November 15, 2000

The other side of the street

Just when we imagine that we have you figured out
you show up working the other side of the street
in your frightening freedom.
You meet us behind and before
as promise and as threat,
and we are overmatched whenever we sit to deal with you.
So we bid you to pay less vigorous attention to us
and we bid you to give us the freedom and courage
that we may withstand you
in ways that are proper to you and to us.
We pray in the name of the utterly humble One
whom you therefore exalted.
Give us wisdom and freedom
that we may sense the ways in which we may best live in this world
where the last become first and the first become last. Amen.

1994

Not at our beck and call

We call out your name in as many ways as we can.
We fix your role towards us in the ways we need.
We approach you from the particular angle of our life.
 We do all that, not because you need to be identified,
 but because of our deep need,
   our deep wound,
   our deep hope.
And then, we are astonished that while our names for you
 serve for a moment,
 you break beyond them in your freedom,
 you show yourself yet fresh beyond our utterance,
 you retreat into your splendor beyond our grasp.
We are — by your freedom and your hiddenness —
 made sure yet again that you are God . . .
  beyond us, for us, but beyond us,
  not at our beck and call,
  but always in your own way.
We stammer about your identity,
  only to learn that it is our own unsettling
  before you that wants naming.
Beyond all our explaining and capturing and fixing you . . .
  we give you praise,
  we thank you for your fleshed presence in suffering love,
  and for our names that you give us. Amen.

On God's Nouns / July 19, 2000

You sweep away what we treasure

Our salute to you tumbles out:
     Lord, sovereign, governor, king
          political images of us before you, gender specific,
          marked by macho.
     Sometimes we speak the terms glibly, out of habit.
     Sometimes we speak them with gravity, counting on you.
But sometimes we are brought up short to see,
                         yet again,
     that you are not kidding: you are other than us.
               you will not be mocked.
Lord, sovereign, governor, king:
     In your will you sweep away what we treasure,
     We watch . . . and you sweep away a range of our idolatries,
          apartheid . . . but not yet our racism,
           military regimes . . . but not yet our superpower,
           heresies . . . but not yet our self-indulgence.
You, you who sweep away and purge,
     Sweep yet the systems of disobedience all around us,
     sweep yet the networks of self-securing we treasure,
     sweep yet our own childhoods that trap us,
     sweep yet our little loves that disable us,
     sweep yet our little fears that rob us of you,
     sweep yet and make new.
Do your Friday sweep yet again, and
suit us for your Sunday governance. Amen.

With 1 Samuel 12:25 / March 30, 2000

No more sinking sand

God of heaven and lord of earth,
Tamer of heaven, lover of earth,
    sovereign over the waters that surge,
    provider for birds, beasts, and fish,
    chooser of Israel and commander of all humanity.
Your vistas remind us
    of how close and small we keep our horizons,
    how much we blink at your power, and wince from your justice,
    how much we waver in the face of your commanding mercy.
You, you, you only, you, God of heaven and lord of earth.
Comes the rain upon our parade,
    and the floods upon our nations,
    and the winds upon our personal configurations,
Comes your shattering and your reconfiguring
    in ways we doubt or we fear.
    We discover yet again, how sandy we are,
    with the quaking of our foundations
        and our fantasized firmaments.
    We are filled with trembling and nightmares that disturb.
And then you-rock-solid-stable-reliable-sure
    You rock against our sand,
    You rock of ages,
    You rock that is higher than us treading water,
    You rock of compassion —
        be compassionate even for us, our loved ones
            and all our needy neighbors,
    You rock of abidingness for our sick,
        and for those long loved, lingering memories,
            dead and in your care,
You rock of justice for the nations,
        fed up with our hate,
            exhausted by the greed of our several tribes,
    You rock of communion in our loneliness,
        rock of graciousness in our many modes of gracelessness.

Come be present even here and there, and there and there,
　　Move us from our sandy certitudes to your grace-filled risk,
　　Move us to become more rock-like
　　　　in compassion and abidingness and justice,
　　Move us to be more like you in our neighborliness
　　　　and in our self-regard.
Yes, yes, yes — move us that we may finally
　　stand on the solid rock, no more sinking sand.
God of heaven. Lord of earth,
　　hear our resolve, heal our unresolve,
　　that we may finish in sure trust and in glad obedience.
　　　　We already know what to do by our careful pondering
　　　　of you. Amen.

After reading Matthew 7:24-29 / September 30, 1993

Before the day is out

Unwavering in your power,
Unflagging in your zeal,
Uncompromising in your position,
 It is good for us — just past Sabbath again,
   just past Easter again —
 to awaken to your will of constancy for your world.
We pursue our projects,
 depart to our private dreams,
 invest in our deepest hopes.
 They are fragile and flimsy at best,
 at worst they are devious and destructive.
 Either way, they pale before your constancy.
We gladly affirm — past our own inclinations —
 that you will well-being among us,
 that you intend justice for the vulnerable,
 that you command mercy and compassion among us.
Turn us, before the day is out, from our will to yours,
Wean us, before we sleep, from our petty hopes,
Relocate us in your eternal resolve,
 that the earth may be fully your realm,
 that the world may wreak with your *shalom*,
 that we ourselves may find our true freedom
  in your sovereign purpose.
Yours — not ours — is the Kingdom, the Power, and the Glory . . .
  and we are grateful. Amen.

Old Testament theology, D. Min. class / July 17, 2000

Three times holy

One time holy,
Two times holy,
Three times holy,
  All cry, "Holy, holy, holy."
You . . . holy,
You . . . unutterable, dread-filled, beyond us . . .
   so unlike us.
We dare glimpse your presence:
   Your holiness testifies to our uncleanness,
   your fierceness tells our apathy,
   your peaceableness notices our pugnacity,
   your generosity bespeaks our stinginess.
So unlike you,
   yet called by you,
   yet sent by you,
   yet authorized by you,
    to hard places,
    to tough times,
    to resistant circumstances.
Called . . . your instruments . . . to the hard places
  that match your holy purposes . . .
    peace, mercy, compassion . . .
    your holy purposes that lead us to that unbearable
     FRIDAY!
Called to Friday as your instruments,
   we are dazzled, more dazzled than grateful. Amen.

On Reading Isaiah 6 / October 9, 2001

The place where you are curbed

We have heard of your wondrous power,
      the ways in which you make newness,
      the ways in which you defeat death,
      the ways in which you give life.
We trust you in the night while we sleep;
we rise early in the morn to find you alert, active, engaged.
You dazzle us day and night.

      Yet . . . we notice the place where
            you are curbed,
            you are fringed,
            you are held.
      Your newness we do not see . . . so we wait.
Keep us easy at night in our wait.
Keep us vigilant in day while we wait.
Keep our wait fixed on you,
            you alone,
            you and none other . . . and we will rejoice. Amen.

On reading 1 Samuel 5 / February 25, 1999

Our true home

God before and God behind,
God for us and God for your own self,
    Maker of heaven and earth,
    creator of sea and sky,
    governor of day and night.
We give thanks for your ordered gift of life to us,
    for the rhythms that reassure,
    for the equilibriums that sustain,
    for the reliabilities that curb our anxieties.
        We treasure from you,
            days to work and nights to rest.
        We cherish from you,
            days to control and nights to yield.
        We savor from you,
            days to plan and nights to dream.
Be our day and our night,
    our heaven and our earth,
    our sea and our sky,
        and in the end our true home. Amen.

Old Testament theology class / November 12, 1998

2

A people with many secrets —
Truth=telling confession

A people with many secrets

You are the God from whom no secret can be hid,
and we are a people with many secrets,
> that we want to tell for the sake of our lives,
> that we dare not tell because they are deep and painful.

But they are our secrets . . . and they count for much;
> they are our truth . . . rooted deep in our lives.

You are the God of all truth,
> and now we bid you heed our truth,
> about which we will not bear false witness . . .

>> The truth of grief unresolved,
>> the truth of pain unacknowledged,
>> the truth of fear too child-like,
>> the truth of hate, as powerful as it is deep,
>> the truth of being taken advantage of,
>>> and being used,
>>> and manipulated,
>>> and slandered.

We trust the great truth of your wondrous love,
> but we will not sit still for it,
> UNTIL you hear us.

Our truth — heard by you — will make us free.
So be the God of all truth, even ours,
> we pray in the name of Jesus,
> who is your best kept secret of hurt. Amen.

Psalms class / January 14, 1999

Like an endless falling

"Things fall apart,
    the center cannot hold."
We are no strangers to the falling apart;
We perpetrate against the center of our lives,
    and on some days it feels
        like an endless falling,
        like a deep threat,
        like rising water,
        like ruthless wind.
But you . . . you in the midst,
        you back in play,
        you rebuking and silencing and ordering,
        you creating restfulness in the very eye of the storm.
You . . . be our center:
        cause us not to lie about the danger,
        cause us not to resist your good order.
Be our God. Be the God you promised,
        and we will be among those surely peaceable in your order.
We pray in the name of the one through whom all things hold together.
                    Amen.

Prayer in class / January 8, 1998

We treasure what you end

We confess that we are set this day in the midst
    of your awesome, awful work.
We will, because we have no alternative,
    be present this day
    to your dreadful work of termination.
We watch while you pull down
    and dismantle
    that with which you are finished.
We will, because we have no alternative,
    be present this day
    to your dream-filled work
    of evoking,
    imagining,
    forming,
    and inviting.
We are double-minded in your presence,
    because we treasure what you end
    and we fear what you conjure —
    but we are your people
    and trust you all this day
    in your awesome,
    awful work.
Override our reluctance
    and take us with you
    in justice
    and mercy
    and peace.
Take us with you in your overriding,
    that our day may be a day of joy
    and well-being
    and newness
    from your very hand.
In the name of your decisive newness,
    even Jesus. Amen.

Loyola University, Bastille Day / July 14, 1989

Not always for you

We yearn, in every season, for your presence;
We know that our hearts will be restless, until they rest in you;
We are like deer who seek a watering hole in the drought;
We hear invitations for "all who are weary and heavy-laden . . ."
        And approach to you seems ready and easy.
Truth to tell, we do pant restlessly,
    but not always for you.
        Sometimes, instead for security
                or sex and beer and sports,
                or power and success,
                or beauty and acceptance . . . not seeking you.
Truth to tell, we know you to be no easy mark,
    with your rigorous entrance requirements
        of blamelessness, truth-telling, no bribes,
        and all manner of neighborliness.
We yearn for you in every season,
    making you too easy, imagining you too difficult,
    bewildered and unsure until you give yourself concretely to us . . .
    as you have done and as you do. Amen.

On reading Psalms 15, 24 / September 19, 2001

You who command

You who command,
You who are our commander,
You who are our commander-in-chief;
  We intend obedience, without reserve.
As we ponder your commands, they often come at us
  like more nagging from our mothers,
  like more rules from our teachers,
  like more expectations from our peers,
  like more pressure from the church,
  like more defeat from our guilty conscience.
Our obedience thins down to resentment,
  tired of the nagging and pressure and rules and expectations.

Then we hear your wonderful words of life,
  and know that in your command is our perfect freedom.

For your command,
for Jesus' glad obedience,
for Jesus' new command of neighbor,
   we give you great thanks.
   We vow full, glad compliance. Amen.

Old Testament theology class / October 20, 1998

We also live double lives

Power turns and postures and exhibits.
    It controls and manages and plots.
        We participate in it,
        we benefit from it,
        we are dazzled by it . . . and more than a little afraid.
Just underneath, all the while . . .
Just underneath dazzling power
        sits violence and brutality,
            greed and fear and envy,
            cunning and shamelessness.
        In that too we participate.
Like the ancients, we also live double lives,
        public in pageant and role and office,
        hidden in meanness and thinness.
We do not do well at bringing this double together.
But we confess you to be Lord of all of our lives.
        Give us new freedom about our public lives,
        give us new candor about our hidden lives,
        Correct what is brutal and greedy and fearful,
        chasten what is hidden and mean.
Make us women and men of *shalom,*
    the kind of welfare you will for our common life. Amen.

On reading 2 Samuel 3 / April 18, 2000

An answering and refusing

We confess you to be the God who calls,
>> who wills,
>> who summons,
>> who has concrete intentions
>>> for your creation,
>> and addresses human agents
>> who do your will.
We imagine ourselves called by you . . .
> Yet a strange lot:
>> called but cowardly,
>> obedient but self-indulgent,
>> devoted to you, but otherwise preoccupied.
In our strange mix an answering and refusing,
> We give thanks for your call.
> We pray this day,
>> for ourselves, fresh vision;
>> for our friends, great courage,
>> for theological students
>>> in places more dangerous than ours,
>>>> deep freedom.
As we seek to answer your call, may we be haunted
> by your large purposes,
We pray in the name of the utterly called Jesus. Amen.

On Reading 1 Samuel 3 / February 20, 2001

Yours, and not ours

You in our past: gracious,
        steadfast,
        reliable,
        long-suffering.
You are a mouthful on the lips of our grandparents.

The hard part is you in our present,
    For after the easy violations we readily acknowledge
    then come the darker, hidden ones:
        aware that appearance does not match reality;
        aware that walk is well behind talk;
        aware that we are enmeshed in cruelty systems
            well hidden but defining;
        and we have no great yearning
            to be delivered from them.
Forgive us for the ways in which we are bewitched,
    too settled, at ease in false places.

You in our present: gracious,
        steadfast,
        reliable,
        long-suffering.
We in the shadows asking you to do what you have done;
            to be whom you have been,
That we may do what we have never dared dream,
    be whom we have never imagined . . .
    free, unencumbered, unanxious, joyous, obedient . . .
    Yours, and not ours. Amen.

On the Penitential Psalms / October 3, 2001

We are takers

You are the giver of all good things.
>All good things are sent from heaven above,
>>rain and sun,
>>day and night,
>>justice and righteousness,
>>bread to the eater and
>>seed to the sower,
>>peace to the old,
>>energy to the young,
>>joy to the babes.

We are takers, who take from you,
>day by day, daily bread,
>taking all we need as you supply,
>taking in gratitude and wonder and joy.

And then taking more,
>taking more than we need,
>taking more than you give us,
>taking from our sisters and brothers,
>taking from the poor and the weak,
>>taking because we are frightened, and so greedy,
>>taking because we are anxious, and so fearful,
>>taking because we are driven, and so uncaring.

Give us peace beyond our fear, and so end our greed.
Give us well-being beyond our anxiety, and so end our fear.
Give us abundance beyond our drivenness,
>and so end our uncaring.

Turn our taking into giving . . . since we are in your giving image:
>Make us giving like you,
>>giving gladly and not taking,
>>giving in abundance, not taking,
>>giving in joy, not taking,
>>giving as he gave himself up for us all,
>>giving, never taking. Amen.

On reading 1 Samuel 8 / March 9, 1999

Fashioning better guarantees

The witnesses tell us that your promises persist
    and will come to fruition;
We find that retelling of such promises deeply compelling
    in our own lives.
      You are the God who reached our family not yet formed.
      You uttered promise and sent father Abraham on his daring way.
      You assured mother Sarah of impossibility
        and sent her laughing in disbelief.
      You hoped them to new land,
        and since have been giving sons and daughters and
          futures and possibilities,
          beyond all that we can hope or imagine.
We are the glad carriers and recipients of those promises.
We live each time from the trace of your future
    that keeps surprising us with
        gifts and chances and hopes.
But your promises seem so flimsy, so risky, so unsure.
      We keep fashioning better guarantees.
      We lie a little here and cheat a little there.
      We add our own securities,
        and then find that every land of promise
        becomes a turf of killing dispute.
      The promise fades; it feels more like we are on our own.
So do this yet today. Match the goodness of your promise
    with the daring of our faith.
      Let us trust beyond seeing,
        risk beyond laughing,
        yield beyond calculating.
By supper time give us the freedom that belongs to your "Yes,"
    Your "Yes" we have seen fleshed in glad obedience. Amen.

On pondering promises / July 13, 2000

The God we would rather have

We are your people and mostly we don't mind,
    except that you do not fit any of our categories.
We keep pushing
        and pulling
        and twisting
        and turning,
    trying to make you fit the God we would rather have,
        and every time we distort you that way
            we end up with an idol more congenial to us.
In our more honest moments of grief and pain
    we are very glad that you are who you are,
    and that you are toward us in all your freedom
    what you have been toward us.
So be your faithful self
    and by your very engagement in the suffering of the world,
    transform the world even as you are being changed.
We pray in the name of Jesus,
    who is the sign of your suffering love. Amen.

In anticipation of reading Jeremiah 4–6 / 2000

But now you know

You are the one from whom no secret can be hid,
who sees behind all of our piety, pretense, and cover-up . . .
    and we are the ones with many secrets,
        some shameful, some shocking, some risky . . .
        all of them precious to us.
We begin this day with that acknowledgment before you,
        you seeing and knowing us,
        a perfect match for our hiddenness.
Those secrets — conventionally — are about
        having done that which we ought not to have done,
        having not done that which we ought to have done.
        And there is enough of that for the day.
Just behind that — other secrets more telling and risky
        and surely more scandalous:
    that behind our ready faith comes impatience with you,
    that behind our eager vocation lurks cynicism,
        because nothing changes,
    that behind our gratitude toward you
        is our sense that you are stingy with us,
    that behind our much prayer is our sureness about your
        absence, indifference, and detachment.
All of that — our deep disappointment in you — is signed
        by our fidelity unappreciated,
        by alienation all around not swamped by your love,
        by loneliness not visited
           in gestures of communion,
        by all the intractable issues of poverty,
           homelessness, and violence
           that we take to be your proper business.
We will keep praying — but now you know.
We will keep praying, but wondering, daring to doubt.
We pray in all our Friday candor. Amen.

On countertestimony / July 20, 2000

Even on such a day

We prattle about your sovereignty . . . especially we Calvinists;
      all about all things working together for good,
      all about your watchful care and your severe mercies.
And then we are drawn up short;
      by terror that strikes us, in our privilege, as insane;
      by violence that shatters our illusions of well-being;
      by death that reminds us of our at-risk mortality;
      by smoke and fire that have the recurring smell of ovens.
We are bewildered, undone, frightened,
      and then intrude the cadences of these old poets:
         the cadences of fidelity and righteousness;
      the sounds of justice and judgment;
         the images of Sodom and Gomorrah;
         the imperatives of widows and orphans.
Even on such a day we are not minded to yield on your sovereignty,
      We are, we confess, sobered, put off, placed in dread,
         that you are lord as well as friend,
         that you are hidden as well as visible,
         that you are silent as well as reassuring.
You are our God. That is enough for us . . . but just barely.
We pray in the name of the wounded flesh of Jesus. Amen.

While reading Isaiah 1 / September 11, 2001

3

Against your absence —
A hidden God

Against your absence

All power, honor, glory be to you!
You . . . sometimes hidden, silent, absent, unresponsive.
We are so privileged that we seldom sense you
        hidden, silent, absent, unresponsive.
But we know people who do,
    we think of places where you do not appear.
We imagine you defeated,
        weak,
        held captive.
And we wait a day,
      two days,
      until the third day.
And then, most often then,
      quite reliably then,
      you appear then in your full glory.
This day we pray against your absence, silence, and hiddenness.
Come with full power into deathly places,
    and we will praise you deep and full. Amen.

On reading 1 Samuel 5 / February 22, 2001

Our despairing hope

Among us are shrivelled women
    who in despair do not eat,
    who in powerlessness weep downcast,
    whose lips tremble, and
    who barely dare ask otherwise.
We in our compassion and sensitivity
    stand alongside those shrivelled women,
    who in despair do not eat,
    who in powerlessness weep downcast,
    whose lips tremble, and
    who barely dare ask otherwise.
Down deep in all candor we ourselves
    are among those shrivelled women;
    we also in despair do not eat,
    we also in powerlessness weep downcast,
    we also have lips that tremble, and
    we also barely dare ask otherwise.
They wait . . .
We wait alongside them . . .
We wait.
And you . . . sometimes . . . speak shalom and the world is made new.
    This day in our despairing hope,
    grant that we, along with all shrivelled women,
    may — before sundown — eat and praise and depart in peace.
For now, we wait. Amen.

On reading 1 Samuel 1:9-28 / February 8, 2001

No newness yet

You are the God who makes all things new.
We gladly raise our voices and move our lips
    to acknowledge, celebrate, and proclaim
        your staggering newness.
As we do so, we hold in our hearts
    deep awareness of all the places where your newness
        is not visible, and
        has not come.
Our hearts link to many places of wretchedness
    short of your newness.
    We picture our folks at home,
        sick, in pain, disabled, paralyzed
        (we name Frank).
        and no newness yet.
    We know up close the deep wretchedness
        of poverty, of homelessness, of hunger
        and no newness yet.
Move our hearts closer to the passion of our lips.
Move our lips closer to your own newness.
Work your newness in hidden, cunning ways among us.
Move us closer to your bodied newness in Jesus,
    newness of strength come in weakness,
    newness of wisdom come in foolishness.
Draw us from the wretchedness we know
    to his scarred, bloody wretchedness
    that is your odd entry of newness into our life.
We pray in the name of his suffering newness. Amen.

Psalms class / January 21, 1999

You are known in hiddenness

God hidden from us in your myriad verbs,
    we confess you where we do not see you:
        in healings,
        in emancipations,
        in feedings,
        in forgiveness,
        in many ways of newness.
We do not see you, but we dare to name you
    by our best names —
        we name you father and mother,
        we make you lord and saviour,
        we praise you giver and lover.
In our daring naming of you and in our very glimpsing,
        we know you are beyond us
                unutterable,
                hidden,
                refusing all our manufactured labels.
You are known in hiddenness,
    powerful in suffering,
    whole in woundedness
And we are yours . . . all of us . . . gladly. Amen.

Old Testament theology class / December 8, 1998

You stay hidden within that misery

God holy, sovereign, faithful, generous —
    that is the first thing we know and affirm at the break of day.
But then, from these old, hard texts we notice
        that your holy, sovereign, faithful generous way with us and
          with our people is in this endless tale of violence . . .
        war, plunder, rape, incest, deception, and death.
You stay hidden within that misery,
            at work even against such circumstance.
We notice that our long-term narrative is just like every other tale,
    wreaking with violence, just like every other . . .
    except for you . . . holy, sovereign, faithful, generous.
We trust your hidden ways today in our narrative
    and in all the narratives of violence in force today.
Work your good will,
         give us eyes to notice what can be seen of you,
         give us faith to trust what stays hidden of you,
         give us nerve to obey you this day,
           even where we do not see.
We pray in the name of Jesus who confounds all our tales of misery.
Amen.

On reading Samuel / October 4, 2000

With or without you

We tell these stories
    about being hungry and thirsty
    and frightened and angry
    and desperate.
And then we tell stories
    about your food and your water
    and your presence.
But the second half of the story
    does not ring powerfully true in our own experience,
    so much so that we find ourselves
    and our whole beloved community
    are often pilgrims in a barren land;
    and we find our sophistication and our affluence
    does not at all treat our condition of wilderness.
So finally we are driven back to you,
    about to receive and then drawn up short
    by the One who has nowhere to lay his head either.
We are bold to pray for your gifts
    and for your presence
    but we do so prepared to endure a while longer
    our thirst and our hunger and our sense of absence
    because we have resolved to be on your way with or without you.
Amen.

1994

Against a closed sky

God of all our times:
>   We have known since the day of our birth
>   that our primal task is to grow to basic trust in you,
>>   to rely on you in every circumstance,
>>   to know that you would return when you are away,
>>   to trust that in your absence you will soon be present,
>>   to be assured that your silence bespeaks attentiveness
>>   and not neglect,
>>   to know that in your abiding faithfulness,
>>>   "all will be well and all will be well."

We do trust in you:
>>   we are named by your name,
>>   and bonded in your service.
>>   We are among those who sing your praise
>>   and who know of your deep faithfulness.

You, you, however, are not easy to trust:
>>   We pray against a closed sky;
>>>   our hopes reduced to auto-suggestion;
>>>   our petitions are more habit than hope;
>>>   our intercessions are kindly gestures of well-being.

Sometimes more, many times not,
>>   because your silence and absence,
>>>   your indifference and tardiness are glaring among us.

We are drawn to find lesser gods,
>>>   easier loyalties,
>>>   many forms of self-trust . . .
>>>   that do not even fool us.

On this Friday of remembered pain and
>>   echoing deathliness,

We pray for new measures of passion,
>   for fresh waves of resolve,
>   for courage, energy, and freedom, to be our true selves . . .
>   waiting in confidence,
>   and while waiting, acting our life toward you
>   in your ways of forgiving generosity.

We pray in the name of Jesus who trusted fully, and
who is himself fully worthy of our trust. Amen.

On reading Jeremiah 17:5-11 / October 26, 2001

4

We are ready to listen —
For illumination

We are ready to listen

Healing, sovereign God,
      overmatch our resistant ears
      with your transforming speech.
Penetrate our jadedness and fatigue.
Touch our yearnings by your words.
Through your out-loudness, draw us closer to you.
We are ready to listen.
Amen.

Illumination / July 9, 1992

Your command is garbled

We imagine you coming into the barracks with your insistent demand.
    We imagine you addressing
        the sun to "move out,"
        the sky — "let there be light,"
        the sea — "stand back."

We imagine you addressing Israel, "be my people,"
        and the church "follow me."

We even imagine you addressing us, each of us and all of us
    with your order of the day.
We imagine . . . but the din of other commands,
        of old loyalties and unfinished business
          and tired dreams
        cause us not to hear well, not to listen, not to notice,
        and your command is garbled.

So come again with your mandate, with the clarity of your imperative.
We listen, because we know in deep ways that your yoke is easy
    and your burden is light.
Come among us, because we are yours, and ours is a listening mood.
Give us ears and then hands and hearts and feet for your good news.
Amen.

Summer school / July 14, 1998

Ears but do not hear

The idols have ears but do not hear . . .
     so unlike you, for all your hearing . . .
     so like us, ears but do not hear.

You have endlessly summoned us: *shema,*
                                          listen,
                                          listen up,
                                          pay attention,
                                          heed,
                                          obey,
                                          turn . . .

We mostly do not . . .   in our narcissism,
                        in our recalcitrance,
                        in our departure from you.

So we pray for ears, open, unwaxed,
                    attentive, circumcised.

Call us by name . . . so that we know,
Call us to you . . . so that we live,
Call us into the world . . . so that we care,
Call us to risk . . . so that we trust
                    beyond ourselves.

You speak / we listen / and comes life,
                    abundant,
                    beyond all that we ask or think . . .
Our ears to hear your word of life.
Amen.

On reading Jeremiah 10:1-16 / March 23, 2000

We would know more of you

You are the God of all truth, the God of deep hiddenness.
    God of all hiddenness who shows yourself in your being hidden,
        who hides yourself in your disclosures,
    we would know more of you
        of your goodness and your mercy,
        of your large purposes and long-term dreams.
In your presence we become aware of how little we know of ourselves,
        of our interests and passions,
        of our fears and dreads,
        of our own wonderments and gifts.
In your truthfulness, let us know more of you
        and in knowing you, ourselves as well.
We pray in the name of Jesus, where we see you fully,
        and ourselves clearly. Amen.

Old Testament theology class / September 29, 1998

The voice we can scarcely hear

You are the voice we can scarcely hear
because you speak to us about dying and suffering,
and we are impacted by so many voices
that have to do with power
and competence
and success.

We do know that you are the voice that gives life,
that you are the voice that opens futures to people who are hopeless.

We are a part of a hopeless people,
because the other voices eat at our hearts,
and we are immobilized
and we become deaf.

So we pray for new ears.

We pray that your voice may be more audible to us,
that we may be able to sort out the death-giving
from the life-giving voices among us.

We pray in the name of Jesus,
through whom you have spoken
in such inscrutable ways.

Amen.

October 1, 1976

The din undoes us

Our lives are occupied territory ...
      occupied by a cacophony of voices,
      and the din undoes us.
In the daytime we have no time to listen,
      beset as we are by anxiety and goals
         and assignments and work,
      and in the night the voices are so confusing
      we can hardly sort out what could possibly be your voice
      from the voice of our mothers and our fathers
      and our best friends and our pet projects,
      because they all sound so much like you.
We are people over whom that word *shema* has been written.
We are listeners, but we do not listen well.
So we bid you, by the time the sun goes down today
      or by the time the sun comes up tomorrow,
      by night or by day,
      that you will speak in ways that we can hear
         out beyond ourselves.
It is your speech to us that carries us where we have never been,
      and it is your speech to us that is our only hope.
So give us ears. Amen.

In anticipation of reading 1 Samuel 2–3 / 2000

The grace to be haunted

As we come to the text,
    we are mindful that we have not come first —
        for others have been there before us.
    We do not come alone —
        for a cloud of witnesses await us.
We give you thanks for the brave people of the text,
    "prophets and apostles, saints and martyrs."
These cadences come easy to us and are familiar.

But if we pray slow,
    we acknowledge before you that there hover around this text:
    prophets — ancient and contemporary —
        who have been truth-tellers at risk.
    apostles — ancient and contemporary —
        sent with passion and courage undaunted.
    saints — ancient and contemporary —
        who have been single-minded for the vision of this text.
    martyrs — ancient and contemporary —
        who have witnessed and suffered and died
            for this particular truth.
And we are their heirs, children, continuers.
    Give us freedom to be in their presence.
    Give us their innocence before the text.
    Most of all, give us the grace to be haunted by them,
                haunted as they were
                    by the text,
                haunted to newness.
We pray in the haunting name of Jesus. Amen.

Day two of summer school / July 11, 2000

Give us Saturday ears

Sometimes it seems as though you have given us
    eyes so that we cannot see,
    and ears so that we cannot hear,
    and hearts so that we cannot know,
    and we miss it.
Work on our ears today.
    Clean them, circumcise them,
    turn them so that they may tingle with the ways
    in which you have turned loose among us the powers of death
    and the forces of life.
Grant that we should not live in the safe middle ground,
    on the surface,
    but push us to the edge,
    where the action is.
Your action, where you cause all those terrible Fridays
    and all those amazing Sundays.
Give us Saturday ears for your tingling.
We pray in the name of your Saturday child. Amen.

In anticipation of reading 1 Samuel 13 / 2000

Reach us

You in your harshness, dismissing,
                    judging,
                    condemning
                    devising evil . . .
You in your mercy, seeking,
                    willing,
                    hoping,
                    wishing,
                    reaching,
                    weeping.
You in your harshness and in your mercy,
You puzzle us,
You bewilder us,
You keep us off balance,
You as you are . . . perhaps because of our fickleness,
                    drive you to extremes,
                    press you to craziness,
                    impel you against your better self.
We in our fickleness, waywardness, hard-heartedness,
            we imagine we are in response,
            but we may be at the outset setting you into vertigo.
We in our empty failure . . . you in bewilderment,
we waiting for your better self . . . you here and there,
                    past vertigo,
                    back in balance, calling and waiting,
                                softly and tenderly,
                                wishing us home
                                    with you.
We yearning to hear your call, afraid to hear,
        because it means return through the mists of harshness,
                    through the risk of mercy,
            in a journey we fear and crave,
                want and dread,
                pledge and renege,
                start and hesitate, in all our double-mindedness.

So reach us with your single-mindedness,
    give us new, single hearts of flesh
    that pulse with praise and trust and obedience,
                with all our heart,
                with all our mind,
                with all our strength, toward you,
                    then our true selves.
We pray in the single-minded name of Jesus. Amen.

On reading Jeremiah 3:1— 4:4 / October 23, 2001

That we may change

Holy God — in this precious hour, we pause
    and gather to hear your word —
to do so, we break from our work responsibilities
    and from our play fantasies;
we move from our fears that overwhelm
    and from our ambitions that are too strong.
Free us in these moments from every distraction,
    that we may focus to listen,
    that we may hear, that we may change.
                            Amen.

Pretoria, South Africa / August 1996

Re-text us

We confess you to be text-maker,
                    text-giver,
                    text-worker,
       and we find ourselves addressed
              by your making, giving, working.
So now we bid you, re-text us by your spirit.
              Re-text us away from our shallow loves,
                     into your overwhelming gracefulness.
              Re-text us away from our thin angers,
                     into your truth-telling freedom.
              Re-text us away from our lean hopes,
                     into your tidal promises.
Give us attentive ears,
       responsive hearts,
       receiving hands;
              Re-text us to be your liberated partners
                     in joy and obedience,
                     in risk and gratitude.
              Re-text us by your word become wind. Amen.

Montreat conference / May 30, 2000

5

Move off the page —
While reading texts

Move off the page

For a week now we have been cast in the role of
        readers,
        students,
        scholars,
        doctors.
A week in the leisure class: air conditioning,
                many books,
                assured food,
                free time
                with only a modicum of anxiety.
In our leisure, we have watched you move from verse to verse,
              noticed the force of your verbs,
              pondered your elliptical textual pauses,
And now we dare interrupt your anticipated sabbath
        with one imperative, for a moment
        not scholars but petitioners in urgency.
So listen up:
      You, majestic sovereign . . . *move off the page!*
                       move off the page to the world,
                       move off the page to the trouble,
                       move out of your paged leisure to
                            the turmoil of your creatures.

Move to the peace negotiations,
      and cancer diagnoses,
      and burning churches,
      and lynched blacks,
      and abused children.
Listen to the groans and moans,
and see and hear and know and remember,
      and come down!
Have no sabbath rest until your creatures rest well, all of us.
Be your Friday self that your world may be Eastered.
      Move off the page!
Amen.

Old Testament theology D. Min. class / July 14, 2000

Before us

Giver of all our years,
ruler of all our times,
>   for this beginning — and all beginnings, we give you thanks.

We pray for energy and freedom and courage
>   proper to a beginning, and ask for your gifts.

While we begin, we acknowledge that
>   we are not, here, not ever, at a beginning.
>   Before us were our mothers and fathers;
>   before us were our teachers and pastors;
>   before us were many scholars who worked hard and saw much,
>   before us were fanatics who have run great risks,
>   and have kept the text for us.

And before all of them, you
>   you in your wisdom and your glory,
>   you in your power and your mercy.

We make our beginning in the presence of all these witnesses,
we make our beginning from you and toward you and in you,
>   that our work and study should be as praise for you,
>   You who give all our years,
>   You who rule all our times. Amen.

Opening class in Old Testament theology / September 10, 1998

We try, as best we can, to live by bread alone

We try, as best we can, to live by bread alone,
> or pie or cake or sweet rolls.
And then comes your word! In our hearing we are reminded that
> we live by every word that proceeds from your mouth,
> promise and gifts,
> blessings and threats,
> summons and commands,
> assurances and requirements.
We thank you for bread, and for the many cakes, pies and sweet rolls
> that inhabit our life of privilege. While we munch,
> give us ears, make us better listeners,
> give us patience with our odd utterances,
> give us openness to your new utterances,
>> we vow to listen.
We pray in the name of your fleshed utterance become our bread.
Amen.

Old Testament theology class / September 24, 1998

You turn tables

Our mothers and fathers have long spoken of you.
And we have their spokenness in our hands, in these old texts.
We propose now to study you,
>> to weigh and test,
>> to examine and assess,
>> to make you our "object" and so to get a grade.
In your strangeness, you are studied only temporarily,
>>>> object only penultimately,
>>>> weighed and tested only at the outset.
But then — as always —
>> You turn tables,
>> You become subject who addresses,
>>>> sovereign who commands,
>>>> mother who loves,
>>>> warrior who defends,
And we find ourselves turned in our study to praise and adoration.
So we ask for freedom to love you with our minds,
>> that we may know a little as we are known,
>> and in knowing may love and adore,
>> and in loving and adoring, may obey . . .
>>>> to your praise,
>>>> and our joy. Amen.

At the beginning of term in Old Testament theology / February 6, 2001

Teach us how to weep

No wonder the prophet weeps yet —
    We begin again, but not innocent . . .
        As we begin, the powers of globalization surge;
            there are victims, but we are mostly beneficiaries.
        There are wars and rumors of wars,
            there are victims, but we are likely perpetrators.
        There is violence, among women, toward the poor,
            violence that refuses to forgive,
            and we are a mix
                of victim and perpetrator.
        The democratic process continues,
            but it is mostly devoid of gravitas,
            and our alarm is modest.
No wonder there is fear, reams of despair, and acres of weeping!
And we feebly watch for you and wait.
    Teach us how to weep while we wait,
        and how to hope while we weep,
        and how to care while we hope.
    Teach us through this strange, ancient, immediate text. Amen.

Beginning the semester with Jeremiah / February 1, 2000

Your world-forming speech

Light from light
Creation from chaos
Life from death
Joy from sorrow
Hope from despair
Peace from hate
      All your gifts, all your love, all your power.
      All from your word, fresh from your word,
      all gifts of your speech.
We give thanks for your world-forming speech.
Thanks as well for our speech back to you,
      the speech of mothers and fathers
          who dared to speak
             in faith and unfaith
             in trust and in distrust
             in grateful memory and in high hurt.
We cherish this speech as we trust yours.
Listen this day for the groans and yearnings of your world,
      listen to our own songs of joy and our own drudges of death,
         and in the midst of our stammering,
            speak your clear word of life
               in the name of your word come flesh.

Amen.

Loyola University, Chicago / July 21, 1989

Your word

Your word is a light to our feet and a lamp to our path.
Your word is a glue of the universe wherein the whole creation coheres.
Your word is the address of promise and command by which we live.
Your word has come fleshed among us full of grace and truth.
     We are creatures of your word and we give thanks for it.
For all that we are more dazzled that your word
     is carried, uttered, acted
     by frail vulnerable human agents.
We ponder and give thanks for those who this day
     speak your word where it is desperately needed
          and deeply resisted.
We ponder and give thanks for those who this day
     act your word for newness and peace and justice.
We ponder with trepidation that among us
     you will yet designate such carriers,
              such speakers,
              such actors.
In our thanks for your word,
     we pray for courage in the name of the one
          who emptied himself. Amen.

In anticipation of reading 1 Samuel 3 / 2000

Our mother tongue

We have learned to speak almost every language except our own.
We are well schooled in the language of hate
                              and of fear
                              and of greed
                              and of anxiety.

We know the language of domination and of excessive deference.
We understand completely the grammar
      of liberalism and conservatism,
                  rhetoric that is revolutionary and reactionary.

But we are strangers in a strange land.
Teach us afresh to trust *our mother tongue* of praise and grief.
We thank you for our speech teachers,
            of many mothers and fathers
                  in many times
                  and many places
                  and many cultures —
                        all of whom know better than do we
                        the ways of truth that heal and of life
                              that enlivens.

Be your true word on our lips and receive our utterances back to you.
We thank you for our mother tongue come in the flesh. Amen.

Prayer in class / January 21, 1988

How you inhabit this text

We confess you to be the creator of heaven and earth;
We are dazzled by your power;
We are encircled by your mercy.
And now we come with this strange text,
     all its jots and tittles,
     all its points and pauses,
Imagining that your splendor is given us in primal ways
     in the detail and nuance of this text.
How you inhabit this text,
How you disclose your hidden self
     through open and closed syllables . . .
     we do not know or comprehend.
We ask for patience, alertness, discernment, and freedom
     as we watch your starchiness
     move from sound to sound.
We give thanks that you have come fleshed in text,
     so powerfully texted are you.
We give thanks in the name of Jesus,
     deeply texted as he was. Amen.

At the beginning of term in Hebrew readings / February 6, 2001

Your new news

The pain is palpable,
    death is close,
the bruises are countless,
       and we are not comforted.
We know about steel against flesh,
    and explosions next to skin,
    and grenades upon bodies,
    and wounds untended,
          infected,
            filled with pus.
    All this is old news to us.
Your new news is
    our flesh next to your presence . . . and so healed,
    our failures next to your body . . . and so transformed,
    our shadowed life next to your generative self . . .
       and so made new.
The cadences dazzle us,
    "made whole by his punishment,
    healed by his bruises."
Your newness bodily overrides our deathliness.
We are staggered by the phrasing,
    so close to us,
    so impossible for us,
    so overpowered by you in your self-giving,
       Fridayed life among us.
"Grateful" is an understatement for how we are toward you. Amen.

On reading Isaiah 52:13—53:12 / April 27, 1999

After the bitterness

It is enough, sometimes, to make one vomit,
        and to have long periods of upset stomach.
Our vomiting over injustice and recalcitrance is a social problem,
        not done in good company.
Your vomiting over arrogance and recalcitrance is more dangerous,
        causing upheavals that shock the markets,
                disturb the peace, and
                destabilize our way in the world.
Give us, after your upset, a better taste;
give us, after your rage, sweetness in our mouths;
give us, after the bitterness, a cup of blessing.
    You are the one who
        takes . . . and blesses . . . and breaks . . . and gives,
                and gives,
                and gives,
                and gives,
                and gives.
We, in the end, receive that Easter cup, and are grateful. Amen.

On reading Jeremiah 25 / May 4, 2000

When the world spins crazy

When the world spins crazy,
        spins wild and out of control
        spins toward rage and hate and violence,
        spins beyond our wisdom and nearly
            beyond our faith,
When the world spins to chaos as it does now among us . . .
We are glad for sobering roots that provide ballast in the storm.
So we thank you for our rootage in communities of faith,
        for many fathers and mothers
           who have believed and trusted
           as firm witnesses to us,
        for their many stories of wonder, awe, and healing.
We are glad this night in this company
        for the rootage of the text,
        for its daring testimony,
        for its deep commands,
        for its exuberant tales.
Because we know that as we probe deep into this text . . .
    clear to its bottom,
        we will find you hiding there,
        we will find you showing yourself there,
                speaking as you do,
                governing,
                healing,
                judging.
And when we meet you hiddenly,
    we find the spin not so unnerving,
    because from you the world again has a chance
        for life and sense and wholeness.
We pray midst the spinning, not yet unnerved,
    but waiting and watching and listening,
    for you are the truth that contains all our spin. Amen.

Lay school on the Pentateuch, after the World Trade Center bombing /
September 17, 2001

The poems conflict us

The intrusion of pain,
the eruption of anger,
the embrace of rage,
and then bewilderment and wonderment and awe.
Our lives in faith are situated among the poets:
The poet talks about,
> swords to plowshares,
> spears to pruning hooks,
> and unlearning war.

But answered by a shadow poet who bids us,
> plowshares to swords,
> pruning hooks to spears,
> be not a weakling! (Joel 3:10)

The poems conflict us, as we are conflicted,
> sensing and knowing better,
> Knowing better, but yielding.

Do not deliver us from the clashing poems
> that are your word to us.

But give us courage and freedom and faith . . . O Prince of Peace.
Amen.

On reading Isaiah 1–2, after the World Trade Center bombing /
September 18, 2001

Soak our lives in it

The realities are as fresh as yesterday,
          as old as our mothers and fathers . . .
    steel and smoke,
    technology and arrogance,
    hate birthed of oppression,
    violence all around,
    violence all around . . . and flesh . . . torn flesh,
                         burned flesh,
                         crushed flesh,
                         lost flesh,
    Steel against flesh, fire searing skin,
    disorder, chaos, confusion, rage, bottomless anxiety.
And we come equipped by our fathers and mothers . . .
    with poetry: surging images,
            two lines of candor,
            openings and closings of praise,
            truth-telling imperatives spoken toward you,
            imagination all voiced to you,
    poetry held deep midst violence,
    poetry of praise midst rage,
    poetry of lament midst loss,
    poetry as wager against hate.
So we pray as we launch into this poetry,
    soak our lives in it,
    overwhelm us by its old cadences,
    speak this poetry on our lips
        that we may echo and shadow and trust
           many mothers and fathers
        for whom this poetry contained the violence.
Utter us through fathers and mothers
    close to You in awe,
    You, the true subject of all our poetry. Amen.

Beginning a class on Psalms, the day after the World Trade Center bombing /
September 12, 2001

Alabaster cities

"Thine alabaster cities gleam,
undimmed by human tears."

We sing unthinkingly of gleaming, alabaster cities,
    We look up "alabaster" . . . "a variety of hard calcite,"
    no help there, and we do not linger,
    but settle for "gleaming":
        bright, shiny steel,
        lights on twenty-four hours a day,
        swift elevators that whisk to the top,
        business, productivity, success, security, power . . .

    . . . undimmed by human tears . . .

        and now dimmed: dimmed by tears,
            blinded by fears,
            wrenched by hate,
            driven by violence,
                very little alabaster,
                even less gleaming,
                lots of tears that dim,
And smoke,
    ashes,
    bodies,
    stench,
    wreckage,
A strange fate for gleaming alabaster.
The great, good cities reduced,
        penultimately we ponder enemies,
        ultimately we are pushed back to you,
            you behind every gleam and every alabaster;
            you behind every ash and every corpse;
            you behind every rage and every tear;
            You finally, keeping watch, hidden;

YOU never to be confused with our gleaming alabaster;
YOU never reduced to our ash and death;
You, living God;
You, Easter God;
You. Amen.

On reading Psalms 46, 74 / October 10, 2001

We are children of another world

For the mystery of the text,
    and for the history of eyes to see
    and ears to hear the text,
        we give you thanks.

Our eyes are scaled
    and our ears are uncircumcised
        and we are children of another world.

We pray for the gift of perception.
We pray for energy and courage,
    that we may not leave the text
        until we wrench your blessing from it.

Amen.

October 18, 1976

6

Awed to heaven, rooted in earth —
For the church in mission

Awed to heaven, rooted in earth

We are the ransomed, healed, restored, forgiven.
We flip off this series of words too readily.
    But they are precious words to us
        because they tell the whole tale
    of our life, and we savor them:
            ransomed . . .   healed . . .
            restored . . .   forgiven.
Made new, made innocent, made possible.
    More than that, these words that tell our truth bind us to you,
and to your passionate truthfulness. While the words linger sweetly
on our lips, we are summoned beyond ourselves — as we always
are — summoned to you, in awe and doxology, and exuberance.
Summoned past ourselves to you . . . only to say . . .
    Alleluia . . . God of heaven;
    alleluia . . . still the same forever;
    alleluia . . . slow to chide,
              swift to bless;
    alleluia . . . gladly all our burdens bearing.
When we sound these ancient cadences, we know ourselves to be at
the threshold with all your creatures in heaven and on earth, every-
one from rabbits and parrots to angels and seraphim . . . alleluia . . .
angels teaching us how to adore you.

AND THEN in the middle of our praise which causes us to float
very light, we are jarred and sobered:
    Dwellers all in time and space . . .
            in time — the beginning of hot summer and not all the
                poor have air conditioners . . . alleluia;
            in time — just days from the Olympics with our worry
                about Coca-Cola, while the homeless urinate and
                evaporate . . . alleluia;
            in place — just near Belfast and the intransigence of fear
                . . . alleluia;
            in place — just near Hebron where the pot of old
                resentments boils to the rim . . . alleluia;

dwellers then in time and place
here, near Atlanta, Belfast, Hebron, and "inside the
beltway" where you are so weak and vulnerable.
That is how it is when we praise you. We join the angels in praise,
and we keep our feet in time and place . . . awed to heaven,
rooted in earth. We are daily stretched between communion
with you and our bodied lives, spent but alive, summoned and
cherished but stretched between. And we are reminded that
before us there has been this One *truly divine* (at ease with the
angels) *truly human* . . . dwellers in time and space. We are
thankful for him, and glad to be in his missional company.
Alleluia. Amen.

After "Praise My Soul," new version, Presbyterian Hymnal 479 / June 24, 1996

Not the God we would have chosen

We would as soon you were stable and reliable.
We would as soon you were predictable
    and always the same toward us.
We would like to take the hammer of doctrine
    and take the nails of piety
    and nail your feet to the floor
    and have you stay in one place.
And then we find you moving,
    always surprising us,
    always coming at us from new directions.
Always planting us
      and uprooting us
      and tearing all things down
      and making all things new.
You are not the God we would have chosen
    had we done the choosing,
    but we are your people
    and you have chosen us in freedom.
We pray for the great gift of freedom
    that we may be free toward you
    as you are in your world.
Give us that gift of freedom
    that we may move in new places
    in obedience and in gratitude.
Thank you for Jesus
    who embodied your freedom for all of us. Amen.

In anticipation of Jeremiah 8–9 / 2000

Re-brand us

You mark us with your water,
You scar us with your name,
You brand us with your vision,
    and we ponder our baptism, your water,
                your name,
                your vision.
While we ponder, we are otherwise branded.
    Our imagination is consumed by other brands,
        — winning with Nike,
        — pausing with Coca-Cola,
        — knowing and controlling with Microsoft.
Re-brand us,
     transform our minds,
            renew our imagination.
     that we may be more fully who we are marked
        and hoped to be,
     we pray with candor and courage. Amen.

Baptism class / September 17, 1998

And we are different

We are counted your people.
　　　We are grateful to be called by you, and
　　　　　glad for our special way of faith in the world.
You have marked us and named us and signed us,
　　　and we are different,
　　　　　　　different memories,
　　　　　　　different hopes,
　　　　　　　different fears,
　　　　　　　different commands,
　　　　　　　different ways of being.
That difference we find glorious, but at times a burden too severe.
　　　We yearn to be like the others,
　　　　　　　like the others in power,
　　　　　　　　　in money,
　　　　　　　　　in freedom,
　　　　　　　　　in certitude,
　　　　　　　　　in security,
　　　　　　　like the others,
　　　　　　　　　uncalled, unburdened, unembarrassed.
We come to you in that deep trial of difference and likeness.
　　　Engage us in our difference,
　　　Give us courage for our different vocations,
　　　　　and energy for our different hope.
In the name of your crucified, Easter One, so unlike all the others.
Amen.

On reading 1 Samuel 8 / March 11, 1999

A hard, deep call to obedience

You are the God who makes extravagant promises.
We relish your great promises
> of fidelity
>> and presence
>> and solidarity,
>> and we exude in them.
Only to find out, always too late,
> that your promise always comes
>> in the midst of a hard, deep call to obedience.
You are the God who calls people like us,
> and the long list of mothers and fathers before us,
>> who trusted the promise enough to keep the call.
So we give you thanks that you are a calling God,
> who calls always to dangerous new places.
We pray enough of your grace and mercy among us
> that we may be among those
> who believe your promises enough
>> to respond to your call.
We pray in the one who embodied your promise
> and enacted your call, even Jesus. Amen.

In anticipation of reading Jeremiah 1–2 / 2000

Yes

You are the God who is simple, direct, clear with us and for us.
You have committed yourself to us.
You have said *yes* to us in creation,
> *yes* to us in our birth,
> *yes* to us in our baptism,
> *yes* to us in our awakening this day.

But we are of another kind,
> more accustomed to "perhaps, maybe, we'll see,"
> left in wonderment and ambiguity.

We live our lives not back to your *yes*,
> but out of our endless "perhaps."

So we pray for your mercy this day that we may live *yes* back to you,
> *yes* with our time,
> *yes* with our money,
> *yes* with our sexuality,
> *yes* with our strength and with our weakness,
> *yes* to our neighbor,
> *yes* and no longer "perhaps."

In the name of your enfleshed *yes* to us,
> even Jesus who is our *yes* into your future. Amen.

Summer school / July 15, 1998

We do not want to be arrested

There is, we discover late and often,
    an arresting quality about your word to us.
    We do not want to be arrested or even pause,
      for our days are planned out.
    And certainly we do not want to be arrested
      by the authorities,
          not for speeding,
          not for trespassing,
          not for shop-lifting,
          Surely not for truth-telling.
Minister to us in our cowardice and timidity.
Set us to be as bold as you are true,
      to meet the authorities who resist and arrest . . .
          our ancient mothers,
          our old convictions,
          powerful ordaining committees,
          and last, even, city hall.
We bid mercy for those of our faith
    who this day are arrested for truth-telling;
Your word is truth, and we live by it,
      frightened or bold,
      free or not,
      in the manner of His own life among us.
      Amen.

On reading Jeremiah 26 / March 7, 2000

Do not fear

We are fearful folk, and we dwell in the midst of a fearful people,
> fearful of our world falling apart,
>> in terror and moral decay,
> fearful of too many "dangers, toils, and snares,"
> fearful of not doing well,
>> of being found out,
>> of being left out,
>> of being abandoned,
>> of our own shadow.
And then we hear, astonishingly in the midst of our fearfulness,
> your mighty, "DO NOT FEAR"
> do not fear, I am with you,
>> with you in wealth and in poverty,
>> with you in success and in failure,
>> with you for better or for worse.
We hear, we trust, we receive your comfort and are made new.
We thank you for the newness of our identity,
> of our trust, of our calling.
Because of your new utterance of life to us,
> we will not fear,
>> though the earth should change,
>> though the mountains shake in the heart of the sea.
We, your new people, thank you for your newness and notice that
you work newness among us, for we know about being,
> lame people who walk,
> blind people who see,
> dead people who live,
> poor people who are unburdened.
We rally round your newness that is both our hope and our work.
Your fearless newness into which we are immersed
> is beyond our expectation;
>> But we are not offended by it;
>>> not scandalized by you;
>>> not ashamed of your newness;
>>> not embarrassed by your healings.

We ask now for energy and freedom, rooted in your fearlessness, that we may live toward and from and for your newness that bubbles up, even in the midst of us, all around us to the uttermost parts of the earth.

We pray in the name of your fearless gift of newness who scandalizes the world and makes all things new, even Jesus. Amen.

Chapel, Isaiah 43:1-7; Luke 7:18-23 / September 17, 1998

Give us appropriate yielding

God of our mothers and fathers long gone and treasured,
God of our grandchildren yet to be and awaited,
God of our years, our days, and even of this moment:
     Our lives are deeply rooted in miracles before us,
     Our faith is richly set in courage running thick,
     Our vocation is shaped by all those
          who have risked for your purposes.
And now, in our remembering, we are made mindful
        of our own place of call, and
        our own time of obedience.
We pray for ourselves and for your whole church,
        courage beyond our easier timidity,
        vision beyond our present tense,
        restlessness beyond our ready settlements, and
        yielding beyond our will to manage.
Give us appropriate yielding that we may be like our remembered
ones in freedom and in love for you. We pray in the name of Jesus
whom we remember until he comes again. Amen.

Campbell scholars, Isaiah 51:1-3; Hebrews 11:8-12, 17-22 / October 26, 2000

We are much drawn to circuses

We reckon bread and circuses is a good political routine.
We are much drawn to circuses,
    and we imagine that we own the bakery.
On our own we do not want to choose between guns and butter,
    so deliver us from all the guns,
    all the butter,
    all the circuses,
    all the bread that we bake.
Give us the leanness to understand and receive and celebrate
    the few nourishments for our common life
    that come from you
    that is all we need.
So override our anxieties about what we shall eat
    and what we shall drink
    and what we shall wear
    and where we shall live
    and what we will save
    and how we will spend
    and what we shall have
    that in intentional and visible and public ways
    we may live as befits your liberated partners.
We pray in the name of Jesus who,
    as far as we know,
    never went to the circus.
Amen.

1994

Our right names

You God toward whom we pray and
    about whom we sing, and
    from whom we claim our very life.
In your presence, in our seasons of ache and yearning and honesty,
    we know *our right names.*
      In your presence we know ourselves to be aliens and strangers.
      We gasp in recognition, taken by surprise at this disclosure,
        because we had nearly settled in
        and taken up residence in the wrong place.
      For all of that, we turn out to be
      we *strangers,* unfamiliar with your covenant,
        remote from your people,
        at odds too much with sisters and brothers,
      we *aliens,* with no hope
        without promise
        with very little sense of belonging or knowing
        or risking or trusting,
      It is in your presence that we come face to face with our beset,
      beleaguered existence in the world.
BUT
      You are the one who by your odd power
        calls us by new names that we can
          receive only from you and
          relish only in your company.
      You call us now,
        citizens . . . with all the rights and privileges and
        responsibilities pertaining to life in your commonwealth.
      You call us now *saints*, not because we are good or gentle
        or perfect,
          but because you have spotted us and marked us
          and claimed us for yourself and your purposes.
      You call us *members* . . . and we dare imagine that we belong
        and may finally come home.
      So with daring and freedom,

we move from our old names known too well
                to the new names you speak over us,
             and in the very utterance we are transformed.
In the moment of utterance and transformation, we look past
        ourselves and past our sisters and brothers here present. And
        we notice so many other siblings broken, estranged, consumed
        in rage and shame and loneliness, much born of wretched
        economics. We bid powerfully that you name afresh all your
        creatures this day, even as you name us afresh. We pray for
        nothing more and nothing less than your name for us all,
                utterly new, restored heaven and earth.
And we will take our new names with us when we leave this place,
        treasuring them all day long,
                citizen,
                saint,
                member,
even as we take with us the odd name of Jesus. Amen.

After reading Ephesians 2:11-22 / undated

Be our primary disease

Be our primary disease,
     and infect us with your justice;
Be our night visitor,
     and haunt us with your peace;
Be our moth that consumes,
     and eat away at our unfreedom.
Be our primary disease,
     our night visitor,
     our moth
          infect, haunt, eat away . . .
Until we are toward you and with you and for you,
     away from our injustice,
          our anti-peace,
          our unfreedom.
More like you and less like your resistance.
     In the name of the one most like you,
               most with you,
               most for you . . . even Jesus.
     Amen.

Prayer in class / January 20, 1998

The anguish and burden of the message

We've never met a Friday we didn't like.
You probably never met a Friday you liked very much
    with all the groaning and anguish and dying there is to be done.
This day we remember and ask your mercy
    upon all our brother and sister pastors
    for whom Friday begins not a weekend
    but one more time the anguish and burden of the message.
And when all the pastors of the Church stand and face
    the seduction and temptation of complacency
    we pray for them, as for us, an unencumbered day
    that they, and in their wake we,
    may learn to speak more clearly
    because we love you more dearly.
Amen.

1994

With all the graciousness we can muster

God of our times, our years, our days.
    You are the God of our work,
        of our rest,
        of our weariness.
Our times are in your hands. We come to you now
    in our strength and in our weakness,
    in our hope and in our despair,
    in our buoyancy and in our disease.
We come to pray for ourselves and for all like us
    who seek and yearn for life anew with you and from you
        and for you.
We pray to you this day, for ourselves and others like us in our *greed*.
    We are among those who want more,
        more money, more power, more piety, more sex,
        more influence, more doctrine, more notice,
            more members,
        more students, more morality, more learning, more shoes.
    Be for us enough and more than enough,
    for we know about your self-giving generosity.
We pray to you this day, for ourselves and others like us
    in our *disconsolation*.
    We are not far removed from those without,
        without love, without home, without hope,
        without job, without health care.
    We are close enough to vision those who must
        check discarded butts to see if there is one more puff,
        who must rummage and scavenge for food,
        for their hungers are close to ours.
    Be among us the God who fills the hungry with good things,
            and sends the rich away empty.
We pray to you this day, for ourselves and others like us
    who are *genuinely good people*,
    who meditate on your Torah day and night,
    who are propelled by and for your best causes,
    who are on the right side of every issue,

who wear ourselves out in obedience to you,
        and sometimes wear others out with our good intentions.
Be among us ultimate enough
        to make our passions penultimate,
        valid but less than crucial.
We are your people. We wait for you to be more visibly
        and palpably our God.
So we pray with our mothers and fathers, "Come, Lord Jesus."
We wait for your coming with all the graciousness we can muster.
Amen.

Prayer in chapel / January 27, 1998

Deliver us from amnesia

God of peace,
God of justice,
God of freedom,
    We give you thanks for your cadences of
        peace, justice, and freedom,
    Cadences that have surged through the lives
        of Martin,
        and Ralph,
        and Rosa,
        and John,
        and Fred,
        and Hosea,
        and Jesse,
        and Andy,
and all that nameless mass of risk-takers who have been
        obedient to your promises
        and susceptible to your dreams.
Deliver us from amnesia
    concerning their courage in the face of violence,
        their peace-making against hate,
        and their hunger for you in a devouring economy.
Deliver us from amnesia:
            turn our memory into hope,
            turn our gratitude into energy,
            turn our well-being into impatience.
That these same cadences of your will may pulse even among us.
Amen.

Martin Luther King Day, a day after / January 19, 1999

Demanding all, not too much, but all

We are covenant makers:
      We make all kinds of vows, oaths, and promises,
      We commit ourselves and practice fidelity,
      We sign on for obedience.
We sign on seriously, but also casually and too easily.
We find ourselves, too soon and too often,
      allied with earthliness: We pant after commodities,
                        We look for quick fixes.
                        We lust after pure well-being.
We look our partners in the face,
      staring at us too often is death, as partner,
      our partner too often too dread-filled to bear.
And then you come, our true and only partner,
                You snatch us from deathliness,
                you nullify our phony covenants,
                and invite us to our proper fidelity.
We look back in wonderment to deathly partners overcome by you.
We look forward in joy to life with you.
We are betwixt and between what was in earthliness
      and what will be in new life;
In that moment of turn, we glimpse life with you,
                life simple, joyous, obedient
                demanding all, not too much, but all.
Amen.

On reading Isaiah 25, 28 / October 30, 2001

Kingdoms rage ... and we are called

Kingdoms rage;
empires tremble;
cities totter.

> You speak assurance;
> You designate human agents;
> You say, "This is my beloved son";
> You say, "This is my anointed."

Right in the middle of chaos,
you designate human agents who do your will.
And we are not sure:

> We would rather it were you,
>
> > directly
> > straight on and visible.

But you stay hidden in your holy splendor,

> and we are left with human agents
> about whom we are never sure.

So we name Jesus, "son of David";

> so human and frail, even if kicked upstairs;
> so vulnerable, even if transformed in song and creed.

And then, in a flash, it may dawn on us:

> You call and designate people like us, your agents.

Kingdoms rage ... and we are called.
Empires tremble ... and we are designated.
Cities totter ... and we are summoned ...

> like the first David, like the second David ...
> us, vulnerable, frail, anxious, your people.
> And we are dazzled. Amen.

On reading Samuel / October 3, 2001

Move us beyond ourselves

Holy God who calls the worlds into being,
      who calls us into Christ's church;
   we thank you for the church that is our true home,
         for the mission of the church that is our true joy, and
         for the ministry of the church that is our proper task.
We thank you for the ministry of the church in this place,
      for pastors and people who over time
        have named your name
        and lived your life.
We thank you for the ministry of the United Church of Christ,
      for its steadfastness over time,
      for its faithful witness in the struggle
        for justice and peace, and
      for its durable walk in caring ways.
We thank you for the ministry to which you have called Rebecca,
      for the caring, eloquent, attentive ways
        in which she will live it,
      for her nurturing church tradition that brought her to faith
        and called her to maturity, and
      for her family that has prayed and believed
        and cared for her
        to this day and this hour.
We thank you for the many ways of ministry that are faithfully
practiced in praise of you out beyond our range of acceptance,
      for those more radical than us,
      for those more cautious than us,
      for those in traditions strange to us,
      for faith families who care in ways other than our own.
We pray this day for all those who stand in need of ministry:
      for the sick and the dying,
      for the powerful who are bewildered,
      for the poor who lack so much we take for granted.
      for the brutalized who wait for relief.
We pray your mighty spirit upon us,
      that we may more fully engage our baptism,

that we may accept the costs
that belong to our life with you,
that we may embrace the joys that only you can give.
Move us beyond ourselves, our favorite cliches,
our tired resentments,
our worn habits,
to your newness.
Make us light, make us ready, make us open,
that we may become a resounding doxology
through your passion and into your victory.
We pray in the name of Jesus crucified, the lord of the church.
Amen.

For the ordination of Rebecca Gaudino / November 10, 1996

7

Start again — For a bruised world

Start again

You are the One who has brought our Lord Jesus Christ
    again to life from the dead;
You are the One who by your summoning imperative
    has caused the worlds to be;
You are the One who by your faithfulness
    has given a son to our vexed mother Hannah;
You are the One who has the will and power to begin again,
                to start anew.
You are the only self-starter whose name we know.
    And so we bid you, start again,
            start here, start now,
            start with us and with our school,
            start with your mercy,
                and with your justice,
                and with your compassion,
                and with your peace.
Make the world new again, and young again, and innocent again . . .
    Start . . . before it is too late. Amen.

On reading 1 Samuel 1 / February 4, 1999

The threats do not wane

The threats do not wane,
The dangers are not imagined,
The power to undo is on the loose . . .
       And in the midst, you speak your word.
It is your word that cuts the threat,
            that siphons off the danger,
            that tames the powers.
You speak and all is made new.
You speak your true self of abiding faithfulness,
             of durable presence,
             of long-standing reliability.
You give yourself in the utterance of "fear not,"
              and we do not fear.
              We do not fear,
              because you are with us,
                 with us, and so safe,
                 with us, and so free,
                 with us, and so joyous.
We diminish our lives in our feeble anxiety . . .
             and you veto our anxiety;
We cheapen our neighbor with our frantic greed . . .
             and you nullify our greed with your satiation;
We pollute our world in our lust for safety . . .
             and you detoxify our mess.
Now come here and in Kosovo,
        here and in Littleton,
        here and in East Lake,
        here and in Louisville,
        here . . . and there . . . and there . . . and there.
Override the fickleness of it all,
     And give us faith commensurate with your true, abiding self.
Amen.

On reading 2 Samuel 7 / April 29, 1999

Their plowshares are beat into swords

And now their plowshares are beat into swords — as are ours.
  now their pruning hooks are beat into spears — as are ours.
    Not only swords and spears,
      but bullets, and bombs, and missiles,
        of steel on flesh,
        of power against bodies . . .
And you, in your indignation sound your mantra,
    "Blessed are the peacemakers."
    We dare to believe they are the aggressor,
        and we are the peacemaker.
    Yet in sober night dream, we glance otherwise
        and think we may be aggressor,
        as we vision rubbled homes,
              murdered civilians,
              and charred babies.
And you, in our sadness, sound your mantra,
    "Blessed are the peacemakers."
    We do not love war,
    we yearn for peace,
        but we have lost much will for peace
        even while we dream of order.
And you, in your hope, sound your mantra,
    "Blessed are the peacemakers."
    Deliver us from excessive certitude about ourselves.
    Hold us in the deep ambiguity where we find ourselves,
    Show us yet again the gaping space
        between your will and our feeble imagination.
Sound your mantra with more authority,
        with more indignation,
        through sadness,
        in hope . . . "Blessed are the peacemakers."
Only peacemakers are blessed.
        We find ourselves well short of blessed.
    Give us freedom for your deep otherwise,
    finally to be blessed,

in the name of the Peacemaker
who gave and did not take. Amen.

For the bombing in Serbia / March 25, 1999

Reform our deformed lives

The words are familiar to us and we are filled with yearning.
So we say them glibly, passionately, filled with hope —
>   liberty, mercy, freedom, release, grace, peace.
We have some fleeting notion of what we must have
>   in order to live our lives fully.
And we have some wistful certitude that these gifts
>   are given only by you,
>   you with the many names . . .
>   you . . . holy, merciful, just, long-suffering, forgiving,
>   >   demanding, promising.
We gather ourselves together to subsume our hopes
>   under your rich names.

We name you by your name, *harbinger of liberty:*
hear our prayers for liberty.
>   We are mindful of those caught, trapped, held, imprisoned
>   by systems of enslavement and abuse, by ideas and
>   ideologies that demean and immobilize, by unreal hopes
>   and ungrounded fears. We ourselves know much of
>   un-liberty, too wounded, too obedient, too driven, too
>   fearful. Be our massive way of emancipation and let us
>   all be "free at last."

We name you by your name, *power of peace:*
hear our prayers for peace.
>   We dare ask for the middle wall of hostility to be broken
>   down, between liberals and conservatives in the church,
>   between haves and have-nots, between victims and
>   perpetrators, between all sorts of colleagues in this place,
>   and in all those arenas besot with violence, rage, and hate.
>   We know we are not meant for abusiveness, but we stutter
>   before our vocation as peacemakers. Transform us beyond
>   our fearfulness, our timidity, our excessive certitude, that
>   we may be vulnerable enough to be peacemakers, and so
>   to be called your very own children.

We name you by your name, *fountain of mercy*:
hear our prayer for mercy.

>Our world grows weary of the battering and the vicious
>cycles that devour us. We seem to have no capacity to break
>those vicious cycles of anti-neighborliness and self-hate.
>We turn, like our people always have, to you, single source
>of newness. Waiting father, in your mercy receive us and
>all our weary neighbors. Remembering mother, hold us and
>all our desperate friends. Passionate lover, in your mercy
>cherish all our enemies. Gift giver, in your mercy embrace
>all those who are strangers to us, who are your well-beloved
>children. Make us, altogether, new.

Hear our prayers for liberty, for peace, for mercy.
>Form us in freedom and wholeness and gentleness.
>>Reform our deformed lives toward
>>obedience which is our only freedom,
>>praise which is our only poetry,
>>and love which is our only option.

Our confidence matches our need, so we pray to you. Amen.

Columbia Theological Seminary / January 13, 1994

Work your wonders

Liberator, Redeemer, Emancipator
       (The terms roll easily off our lips.)
   For your power that notices,
      your passion that descends,
      your freedom that liberates,
   We thank you.
We hold in your presence all those bondaged,
      in fear and despair,
      in poverty and weariness,
      in crime, war, and violence,
      in narcissism and self-indulgence.
Work your wonders among us,
      in your strength like war,
      in your gentleness like nursing,
      in your abiding love like forever.
Work your wonders,
      we pray in the weak name of Jesus. Amen.

Old Testament theology / October 13, 1998

In the midst of all the pushing and shoving

In the midst of all the pushing and shoving
        among us,
        in the world and in the church,
        propelled by anxiety and
        acted as brutality,
You have planted yourself in all your fidelity.
You have placed yourself among us
        in steadfastness and abiding care
        present in the day,
        alert in the night,
        making us all safe and noticed and cared for.
So evidence your fidelity as to curb our anxiety,
                        as to restrain our brutality,
                        as to overcome our alienation.
By your fidelity, renew us,
        renew church,
        renew city,
        renew world.
Give us the safety to love you fully,
        to love neighbor well,
        in glad obedience. Amen.

On reading 2 Samuel 7 / May 4, 1999

Come to our shut down places

It does not come easy to us to imagine that you
        closed the womb of mother Hannah
        and thereby foreclosed the future for a time.
And yet, we can name in your presence
        a myriad of shut-down places around us . . .
            those shut down in poverty and despair,
            those shut down in fear and in rage,
            those shut down by abuse and violence,
        too hurt to speak,
        too frightened to appear,
        too scarred to dance.
And closer, our own shut downs:
        in anxiety, in resentment, in pretense,
            too weary to care,
            too greedy to share,
            too much of us for neighbor.
These are not all your doing, we confess.
But you are the God who opens all shut downs:
        by your power, you give futures,
        by your goodness, you give hope,
        by your mercy, you make new.
So we bid you this day come to our shut down places
        and give birth anew.
We pray through the Easter opening of the Friday shut downs.
Amen.

On reading 1 Samuel 1 / undated

We are all in hock

Christ is risen!
You have come into a world of debt where we are all in hock.
We pray daily that you forgive our debts.
We boldly qualify our prayer by the condition
    of how we treat our neighbors.
So we pray for the cancellation of our debts
        and the debts of the poor,
            of the weak,
            of the imprisoned,
            of the abused.
Your Easter Jubilee has broken our old patterns of debt and credit,
      and made us all rich beyond our acknowledgment.
You are the one who was rich and became Friday poor,
    that by being made poor,
    you would make many rich.
We are among those who have been made rich . . .
    along with our neighbors.
For your Sunday wealth that is our new beginning,
    we give you deep and exuberant thanks.
Amen.

On Jubilee / May 3, 2000

While the world says "not possible"

Holy God who moves this day toward peaceableness,
      God of Jew and Greek   God of male and female,
      God of slave and free,   God of haves and have-nots,
      God of the buoyant and the frightened,
      God of the tax-collector and the Pharisee,
You God who makes all things new!
We come to you this day in dazzled thanksgiving for the reconciliation
        you have wrought in our midst,
      Some we all know . . . the strangeness of Gaza and Jerusalem,
                    . . . the new paths in Capetown and
                         Johannesburg,
                    . . . the thinkably good option in Belfast;
      Some we know secretly, so close to home,
          of transformations and healings and reconciliations
          and the defeat of anger and hate and hurt.
      We are dazzled and grateful, more than we can say.
God of all newness, we come to you this day in daring hope,
      for healings we want yet to receive, believing in them,
         while the world says "not possible"
      We dare imagine . . . healings in Rwanda,
                 . . . and peaceableness in Haiti,
                 . . . and trustfulness close between
                     conservatives and liberals,
                 . . .and caring between those who have so
                     little and those who have too much,
                 . . .healings that can happen
                     only by your good office.
Dear God of our waxing and our waning, we risk uttering
      the groanings of our hearts for reconciliation,
         sighs too deep for uttering,
      we so deeply yearn for, but do not think possible,
      not possible for the homeless and the homed to live together,
        but we groan,
      not possible for homosexuals and heterosexuals of all sorts
        to commune together, but we anguish,

not possible to move past our burdens of fear and brokenness,
    of abuse and weariness, not possible, but we imagine it,
not possible to be innocently alive with all the burdens
    we must keep hidden,
      not possible, but we pray for your impossibility.
God of Exodus and Easter, God of homecoming and forgiveness,
    God of fierceness and peaceableness,
      we are finally driven to your miracles.
This day hear our urgency and do among us
    what none of us can do.
Do your Friday-Sunday act yet again and make us new.
We pray out of the shattering death and the shimmering new life of
    Jesus, whose name we bear. Amen.

Yom Kippur / September 15, 1994

We are not self-starters

Speaking, acting, life-giving God
      the one with the only verbs that can heal and rescue,
We come petitioning one more time,
        Seeking your majestic address to us,
        asking your powerful action among us,
        waiting for your new life toward us.
Your creation teems with bondaged folk
      who have not enough for life,
            not enough bread, not enough clothes,
            not enough houses, not enough freedom,
            not enough dignity, not enough hope.
Your creation teems with bondaged creatures,
         great valleys become dumps,
         great oceans become dumped pollution,
         fish wrapped in dumped oil,
         fields at a loss for dumped chemicals.
So we pray for creation, that has become a dump,
      and for all your people
        who have been dumped,
        and dumped upon.
Renew your passion for life,
Work your wonders for newness,
Speak your word and let us begin again.
      In your powerful presence, we resolve to do our proper work,
But we are not self-starters.
      We wait on you to act, in order that we may act.
Show yourself in ways that give us courage and energy and freedom,
      that we may care for our neighbors,
        love your creation,
        praise your name.
We pray in the savaged power of Jesus,
      who cared and loved and praised.
Amen.

Chapel / February 5, 1990

Be your powerful, active, sovereign self

You are the God who creates and recreates,
 who judges and delivers,
  who calls by name and makes new.
This much we gladly confess in praise and thanksgiving.
This much we trust and affirm . . .
 only to ponder the chance that we are too glib,
  that we say more than we mean,
  that we say more
   than we can in fact risk.
We make our gingerly confession in a world filled
 with those who cynically acknowledge none but themselves . . .
  and we are their fellow travellers
 with those who in vulnerability have no chance
  but prayer to you . . .
   and we stand in solidarity with them.
Thus we ask, beyond our critical reservations,
 that you be your powerful, active, sovereign self.
Give us eyes to see your wonders around us;
Give us hearts to live into your risky miracles;
Give us tongues to praise you beyond our doubt.
 For it is to you, only you, that we turn on behalf of the world
 that waits in its deathliness for your act of life. Amen.

On Von Rad's "Mighty Deeds" / February 20, 2001

Friday is your day of entry

Giver of good gifts, we give you hearty thanks . . . that it is Friday.

We say, without guilt, "Thank God It's Friday!"

Partly, as we come to Friday, along with our culture, we are into *week-ends* of self-indulgence. We have worked hard and are ready to take a break and rest from our labors. We wait for a moment when we need not pay attention to the steady demands with which we live, caring not at all for the world, or for our neighbor, or our duty.

Give us the mercy to move Friday beyond "the week-end." Partly as we move to Friday we are ready *for Sabbath rest,* when we rest as we imagine you to rest. It is clear to us in our best pondering that our lives are made for rest and not for work. So give us the simplicity to put ourselves down in your rest, whereby we may receive back our true selves by drawing close to you.

But mainly, as we come to Friday, we know in our deepest places that *Friday is your day* of entry into the hurt and hate of the world, your day of bottomless weakness where we have seen you allied with the world in its deepest disorder. We know you to be a Friday God without the honors of omnipotence. And so we pray that you will "Friday us" into the very weakness where we may receive our new life from you.

We pray in the name of your Friday Child. Amen.

Prayer in class / January 9, 1998

Into our several hells

There is evidence that our society is going to hell in a handbasket;
The hell holes are easy to spot in the news;
And we, even in our privilege, know various signs and degrees of hell.
But we confess that you are the God
        who has descended into our several hells,
                    submitted,
                    suffered,
                    been present . . .
      and then raised in power to new life.
We care not so much about your ascent into heaven
      as we do about your restoration of the earth.
You are the God who raised others even as you ascend in new power.
    So raise us this day from all our negativities;
    So raise our city this day from its cruel failures;
    So raise our world this day from its several hells
        of brutality and uncaring.
    So raise us to new praise and glad obedience.
You who descend and who are raised in splendor. Hallelujah! Amen.

On reading 2 Samuel 12 / May 2, 2000

Is there a balm . . . in Gilead or anywhere?

We come to your presence haunted by an old question:
    The question is posed by your presence,
        for we would not ask it otherwise.
    The question is an old one,
        asked by our mothers and fathers forever.
    Haunted because we do not know . . . and we must know.
So now yet again, like all our predecessors,
    We ask again,
        Is there a balm . . . in Gilead or anywhere?
        Is there medicine for what ails us?
        Is there healthcare with you, so absent everywhere else?
        Is there a drug to deal with our infection?
        Is there a heavy dose for our pathology?
We ask, linger for your answer, but do not know.
We ask, then rush to lesser remedies, to quack physicians,
                to secret recipes,
                all the while thinking
                    to heal ourselves.
But then back to you, still needing your answer.
      We suspect a "yes" from you,
          We ponder the way you healed old slaveries,
             the way you sent Jesus
                among the disabled,
             the way your spirit has surged to heal.
We crave a "yes" from you and wait.
We wait . . . midst our disabilities of fear and anxiety;
We wait . . . aware of our pathologies of hate and rage and greed;
We wait . . . knowing too well our complicity in violence
    we need not see . . .
        We cut below that . . .
We wait in weariness, in doubt, in loneliness.
And we pray: say the word and we will be healed;
        say the word and our bodies will move to joy;
        say the word and our body politic will function again;
        say the word that you have fleshed in Jesus;

say the word . . . we will wait for your healing "yes."
And while we wait, we will "yes" you with our trusting obedience.
Amen.

On reading Jeremiah 8:18—9:3 / October 23, 2001

Ours is a seduced world

God of all truth, we give thanks for your faithful utterance of reality.
  In your truthfulness, you have called the world "very good."
  In your truthfulness, you have promised,
            "I have loved you with an everlasting love."
  In your truthfulness, you have assured,
            "This is my beloved Son."
  In your truthfulness, you have voiced, "Fear not, I am with you."
  In your truthfulness, you have guaranteed that
            "Nothing shall separate us from your love
                in Jesus Christ."
It is by your truthfulness that we love.
And yet, we live in a world phony down deep
    in which we participate at a slant.
Ours is a seduced world,
      where we call evil good and good evil,
      where we put darkness for light and light for darkness,
      where we call bitter sweet and sweet bitter (Isa. 5:20),
      where we call war peace and peace war,
so that we rarely see the truth of the matter.
Give us courage to depart the pretend world of euphemism,
          to call things by their right name,
          to use things for their right use,
          to love our neighbor as you love us.
Overwhelm our fearful need to distort,
      that we may fall back into your truth-telling about us,
      that we may be tellers of truth and practitioners of truth.
We pray in the name of the One whom you have filled
          with "grace and truth." Amen.

On reading Jeremiah 23 / October 29, 2001

Ceding our end to you

We confess, when we ponder your large governance,
    that our "chief end" is to
    glorify you and enjoy you forever.
We confess that the purpose of our life, purposes twinned,
    are your glory and our joy. That is our true end!
But when we come to the end of our work together, and
        the end of our text together,
It strikes us that we know less about "ends" than we imagine.
    We sing our explanatory doxologies,
    We reiterate our concluding slogan that
        "thine is the kingdom and the glory and the power."
    We add our confident, loud "Amen" to our best petitions.
But—truth to tell—
    We cannot see the end;
    when we do see the end, we do not know its meaning . . .
        whether termination or transition.
And so, like our many fathers and mothers always,
    We trust where we cannot see,
        eating what we are fed,
        taking what of recognition we can muster,
        restless and present under a myriad of surveillances,
        but finally ceding our end to you,
        in our simple, final prayer:
            Come Lord Jesus.
            Come among us,
            Come to your church in bewilderment,
            Come to our state in its vexation,
            Come to our world in its insomnia.
Grant us peace with justice,
    peace with joy,
    peace at the last,
    peace on earth . . . and glory to you in the highest. Amen.

On reading Jeremiah 52:31-34, last day of class / November 2, 2001

8

We will not keep silent —
Cadences of gratitude

We will not keep silent

We are people who must sing you,
    for the sake of our very lives.
You are a God who must be sung by us,
    for the sake of your majesty and honor.
And so we thank you,
    for lyrics that push us past our reasons,
    for melodies that break open our givens,
    for cadences that locate us home,
        beyond all our safe places,
    for tones and tunes that open our lives beyond control
                and our futures beyond despair.
We thank you for the long parade of mothers and fathers
    who have sung you deep and true;
We thank you for the good company
    of artists, poets, musicians, cantors, and instruments
    that sing for us and with us, toward you.
We are witnesses to your mercy and splendor;
    We will not keep silent . . . ever again. Amen.

Psalms class / January 20, 1999

You give . . . and we receive

We are your people . . . like Mother Hannah
    We come with our several eating disorders,
                trembling lips,
                needy hands,
                fallen faces,
                quiet in despair.
    Because we do not have what we need, by ourselves —
    to make a future. And so we ask.
And you give! Generously, abundantly, inexplicably.
    You give more than we ask or think or need,
        enough for all our futures,
        enough for joy,
        enough for well-being beyond our trembling neediness.
You give . . . and we receive.
    We receive and sometimes we covet and own and possess.
    We receive and imagine it is our purchase.
    We receive your good gifts like property.
    We receive and want more.
You give . . . and we receive . . .
    Sometimes we only thank in amazement,
    Sometimes we yield in gratitude.
    Sometimes we turn our joy into sacrifice and give back.
    Sometimes we become more fully yours
        in obedience and gladness.
And now is some such sometime. We pray in thanks. Amen.

On reading 1 Samuel 1 / February 9, 1999

The God who yearns and waits for us

We are strange conundrums of faithfulness and fickleness.
We cleave to you in all the ways that we are able.
We count on you and intend our lives to be lived for you,
   and then we find ourselves among your people
   who are always seeking elsewhere and otherwise.
So we give thanks that you are the God
  who yearns and waits for us,
    and that our connection to you is always from your side,
    and that it is because of your goodness
    that neither life nor death
      nor angels nor principalities
      nor heights nor depths
      nor anything in creation
        can separate us from you.
We give you thanks for your faithfulness,
  so much more durable than ours. Amen.

In anticipation of reading Jeremiah 2–3 / 2000

The gratitude we intend

The witnesses tell of your boundless generosity,
>   and their telling is compelling to us:
>   You give your word to call the worlds into being;
>   You give your sovereign rule to emancipate the slaves
>   and the oppressed;
>   You give your commanding fidelity to form your own people;
>   You give your life for the life of the world . . .
>   broken bread that feeds,
>   poured out wine that binds and heals.
>   You give . . . we receive . . . and are thankful.
We begin this day in gratitude,
>   thanks that is a match for your self-giving,
>   gratitude in gifts offered,
>   gratitude in tales told,
>   gratitude in lives lived.
Gratitude willed, but not so readily lived,
>   held back by old wounds turned to powerful resentment,
>   retarded by early fears become vague anxiety,
>   restrained by self-sufficiency in a can-do arrogance,
>   blocked by amnesia unable to recall gifts any longer.
Do this yet. Create innocent space for us this day
>   for the gratitude we intend.
In thankfulness,
>   we will give,
>   we will tell,
>   we will live,
>   your gift through us to gift the world. Amen.

On today / July 12, 2000

We are second and you are first

Before our well-being, there was your graciousness,
before our delight, there was your generosity,
before our joy, there was your good will.

We are second and you are first.
You are there initially with your graciousness, your generosity,
    your good will —
and we receive from your inscrutable goodness grace upon grace,
    gift upon gift, life upon life
        — because you are there at the beginning,
            at all our beginnings.

For a quick glimpse, we move out beyond our competence,
    our productivity, our self-sufficiency
        — in our new freedom what we glimpse is you —
outpouring yourself unreservedly in the midst of our hurt
    and toward our hopes.
    You are there in the splendor of your self-giving.

So we speak our timid, trembling praise back to you,
    timid because we are no match for your goodness,
    trembling because our praise means turning our life to you,
    and we do not turn loose easily.
        But we do turn loose to you,
            source and goal of our very life.

Our gratitude arises out of the dailiness of our well-being,
    of meals regularly before us, of folks regularly caring for us,
    of homes regularly warm and safe, of sleep regularly refreshing,
    of new days regularly given against the darkness,
    of work regularly filling our days with order and dignity.
And in our taken-for-granted regularity,
    we discern your abiding and fidelity that holds our worlds
    toward well-being.

Our gratitude wells up in the midst of such regularity —
new words spoken, new children born,
new vistas opened, new risks taken,
new words uttered that heal.
We dare confess that in these startling break points,
we glimpse your powerful care
which runs beyond our capacity to manage
and beyond our exhausted capacity to cope.
You . . . after all our best efforts,
it is you, you who hold and you who break.
And we are grateful. Amen.

Myers Park Baptist Church, Charlotte, N.C. / October 21, 1990

With you it is never "more or less"

We will be your faithful people —
                    more or less
We will love you with all our hearts —
                    perhaps
We will love our neighbor as ourselves —
                    maybe.
We are grateful that with you it is
                    never "more or less,"
                              "perhaps," or
                              "maybe."
With you it is never "yes and no,"
          but always "yes" — clear, direct,
          unambiguous, trustworthy.
We thank you for your "yes"
          come flesh among us. Amen.

Old Testament theology class / November 3, 1998

Giver, Giver, Giver

Creator, giver of goodness, creator of all that is . . .

                                 dayenu . . . loaves abound!

Redeemer, giver of new creation . . .

Spirit, multiplier of loaves . . .

We are children of your bounty,

        daughters and sons of privilege . . .

We live midst ample food, ample clothes,

        ample housing, ample cars, ample stereos,

        ample friends, ample security . . .

We have ample and count on it,

        reckoning our luxuries to be necessities . . .

And we are grateful . . .

In our gratitude,

        we notice the war refugees in Kosovo . . .

        we notice the war on poverty,

           even with our government surpluses . . .

        we notice our ample housing

           along with 20,000 in Atlanta on the streets . . .

        we notice how you grace our church

           midst our fear and rage and cunning . . .

        we wonder about our grades

           and our worth and our honor . . .

        we ask about inheriting eternal life . . .

        and turn away with our great possessions . . .

Giver, Giver, Giver who overrides fear in utterance . . .

                who overrides scarcity in abundance . . .

                who overrides parsimony in generosity . . .

                we are among the 5,000 . . .

                we are dazzled by twelve baskets left . . .

Our gratitude does not match your generosity,

        but we are grateful . . .

For all your gifts including the gift of your very own life to us,

we give you thanks . . . Amen. And all the people said . . .

Prayer: "dayenu . . . loves abound!" / October 20, 1998

Larger than fear

We do not really know about running and hiding.
We do not have any real sense, ourselves, of being under assault,
    for we live privileged, safe lives,
    learning in a garden near paradise.
Nonetheless the fear and the prayer
    live close beneath the surface . . .
        enemies we cannot see,
          old threats lingering unresolved from childhood,
          wild stirrings in the night that we cannot control.
And then we line out our imperative petitions,
    frantic . . . at least anxious;
    fearful . . . at least bewildered;
Turning to you, only you, you . . . nowhere else.
In the midst of our anxiety, confidence wells up,
In our present stress, old well-being echoes.
We speak and the world turns confident and grateful,
    not because we believe our own words,
    but because of your presence,
        your powerful, bold, reliable presence
          looms large,
          larger than fear,
          larger than anxiety,
          large enough . . . and in our small vulnerability,
            we give thanks.
                Amen.

On reading Psalm 54 , after the World Trade Center bombing/
September 26, 2001

We notice your giving

You God of command who issues demands upon us;
You God of promise who compels us to hope;
You God of deliverance endlessly up-ending our systems of abuse;
In all your commanding, your promising, your delivering,
 we notice your *giving*.
  Indeed your giving is what we notice first, best, and most,
   about your own life . . .
   giving without reserve or limitation.
You give us worlds of beauty and abundance,
   blessed and fruitful,
You give us sustenance for the day,
    so that we are not smitten by the sun by day
     or by the moon by night.
You give us — in the center of all your giving —
  your only, well-beloved Son.
You give us your spirit of power, energy, and wisdom.
   Gifts all without grudging!
And we receive, because we have no alternative,
   because we cannot live without your gifts,
   because we have nothing but what you have given us.
We receive, carefully and anxiously,
   worried that there is not enough,
    of security and safety,
    of grades or grants or dollars or friends,
    of sex or beer or SUVs,
     or students and endowments,
    of futures, and so we crave and store up
     for rainy futures.
We receive occasionally when you stagger us
  and we break beyond anxiety,
   in gratitude,
    recognizing that you in your generosity give us
     more than enough,
    and in grateful giving we become our true selves,
     breathed in the image of your Son.

So we ponder your generosity and are dazzled.
We measure our gratitude and our capacity to be generous.
We pray your haunting us beyond ourselves,
in wonder at your way,
in love for the world you love,
in praise that transforms our fear,
in wonder, love, and praise,
our lives beyond ourselves,
toward you,
a blessing in the world.
Hear us as we pray in the name of the emptied, exalted One. Amen.

A chapel prayer / September 20, 2001

9

Occupy our calendars —
Praying the Christian year

Occupy our calendars

Our times are in your hands:
　　　But we count our times for us;
　　　　　we count our days and fill them with us;
　　　　　we count our weeks and fill them with our busyness;
　　　　　we count our years and fill them with our fears.
And then caught up short with your claim,
　　　Our times are in your hands!
Take our times, times of love and times of weariness,
Take them all, bless them and break them,
　　　　　give them to us again,
　　　　　　　slow paced and eager,
　　　　　　　fixed in your readiness for neighbor.
　　　　　Occupy our calendars,
　　　　　Flood us with itsy-bitsy, daily *kairoi,*
　　　　　in the name of your fleshed *kairos.* Amen.

Montreat Conference: Jubilee / June 1, 2000

The grace and the impatience to wait

In our secret yearnings
    we wait for your coming,
    and in our grinding despair
    we doubt that you will.
And in this privileged place
    we are surrounded by witnesses who yearn more than do we
    and by those who despair more deeply than do we.
Look upon your church and its pastors
    in this season of hope
    which runs so quickly to fatigue
    and this season of yearning
    which becomes so easily quarrelsome.
Give us the grace and the impatience
    to wait for your coming to the bottom of our toes,
    to the edges of our finger tips.
We do not want our several worlds to end.
Come in your power
    and come in your weakness
    in any case
    and make all things new.
Amen.

1994

In violence and travail

We give you thanks for the babe born in violence.

We give you thanks for the miracle of Bethlehem,
born into the Jerusalem heritage.

We do not understand why the innocents must be slaughtered;
we know that your kingdom comes in violence and travail.
Our time would be a good time for your kingdom to come,
because we have had enough of violence and travail.

So we wait with eager longing,
and with enormous fear,
because your promises
do not coincide with our favorite injustices.

We pray for the coming of your kingdom on earth
as it is around your heavenly throne.

We are people grown weary of waiting.

We dwell in the midst of cynical people,
and we have settled for what we can control.

We do know that you hold initiative for our lives,
that your love planned our salvation
before we saw the light of day.

And so we wait for your coming,
in your vulnerable baby
in whom all things are made new.

Amen.

December 6, 1976

There is a time to be born, and it is now

There is a time to be born and a time to die.
And this is a time to be born.
So we turn to you, God of our life,
    God of all our years,
    God of our beginning.
  Our times are in your hand.
Hear us as we pray:
  For those of us too much into obedience,
    birth us to the freedom of the gospel.
  For those of us too much into self-indulgence,
    birth us to discipleship in your ministry.
  For those too much into cynicism,
    birth us to the innocence of the Christ child.
  For those of us too much into cowardice,
    birth us to the courage to stand before
      principalities and powers.
  For those of us too much into guilt,
    birth us into forgiveness worked in your generosity.
  For those of us too much into despair,
    birth us into the promises you make to your people.
  For those of us too much into control,
    birth us into the vulnerability of the cross.
  For those of us too much into victimization,
    birth us into the power of Easter.
  For those of us too much into fatigue,
    birth us into the energy of Pentecost.
We dare pray that you will do for us and among us and through us
  what is needful for newness.
Give us the power to be receptive,
    to take the newness you give,
    to move from womb warmth to real life.
We make this prayer not only for ourselves, but
    for our school at the brink of birth,
    for the church at the edge of life,
    for our city waiting for newness,

for your whole creation, with which we yearn
in eager longing.
There is a time to be born, and it is now.
We sense the pangs and groans of your newness.
Come here now in the name of Jesus. Amen.

Epiphany: Hosea 13:12-14; John 3:1-21 / January 7, 1997

Not yet as light as hope

We remember the long dark nights of Ashdod;
  They were long because you stood
    in the Philistine place passively;
  They were dark because the gods of the Philistines
    seemed to prevail.
And now we face the long, dark days of Lent:
  to ponder your strange passivity,
  to hold deep the suffering of Jesus,
  to grasp afresh our fragile mortality, that we too will die;
  to move beyond ourselves to notice the raw loss
    connected to your absence.
We name the brutality among us;
We make the greed so close to us;
We see the poor, the homeless, the exploited,
    while we enjoy the easiness of the leisure class.
And then — dark and long — our eyes shift back to Ashdod;
  We wait, a heavy wait edging toward hope,
    not yet as light as hope,
    as heavy as absence.
We pray in the name of the crucified. Amen.

Shrove Tuesday with 1 Samuel 5 / February 27, 2001

Loss is indeed our gain

The pushing and shoving of the world is endless.
> We are pushed and shoved.
> And we do our fair share of pushing and shoving
>> in our great anxiety.
> And in the middle of that
>> you have set down your beloved suffering son
>> who was like a sheep led to slaughter
>> who opened not his mouth.
> We seem not able,
> so we ask you to create the spaces in our life
> where we may ponder his suffering
> and your summons for us to suffer with him,
> suspecting that suffering is the only way to come to newness.
So we pray for your church in these Lenten days,
> when we are driven to denial —
>> not to notice the suffering,
>> not to engage it,
>> not to acknowledge it.
So be that way of truth among us
> that we should not deceive ourselves.
That we shall see that loss is indeed our gain.
We give you thanks for that mystery from which we live.
Amen.

In anticipation of reading 1 Samuel 8 / 2000

Revise our taking

You, you giver!
You have given light and life to the world;
You have given freedom from Pharaoh to your people Israel;
You have given your only Son for the sake of the world;
You have given yourself to us;
You have given and forgiven,
>   and you remember our sin no more.
And we, in response, are takers:
>   We take eagerly what you give us;
>   we take from our neighbors near at hand as is acceptable;
>   we take from our unseen neighbors greedily and acquisitively;
>   we take from our weak neighbors thoughtlessly;
>   we take all that we can lay our hands on.
It dawns on us that our taking does not match your giving.
In this Lenten season revise our taking,
>   that it may be grateful and disciplined,
>   even as you give in ways generous and overwhelming.
Amen.

On reading 1 Samuel 8 / March 1, 2001

Or did we get it wrong

We salute you Prince of Peace
Then we daily commit violence:
    against our neighbor close at hand, by word and deed;
    against our neighbor far away,
        by our systems that keep hurt invisible;
    against creation by our heavy consuming;
        . . . wittingly, unwittingly,
          greedily, without caring.
And then find much of our violence
    is in the name of your righteousness,
        that you have started these cycles of violence
        with your ethnic cleansing.
Or did we get it wrong?
Or did you get it wrong?
Prince of Peace: Purge the hungry violence among us.
        Use this Lent to turn away our devouring habits,
        Make us thin and lean and quiet,
          and led beyond your fierceness.
            Prince of peace!
            Amen.

On reading 1 Samuel 15 / March 27, 2001

In the name of the bruised one

The cadences of suffering love sound in the church in this Holy Week.
We ponder this coming Thursday and
   this ready Friday.
Beating solemnly and transformatively in the foreground is this . . .
   "wounded for our transgressions,
   bruised for our iniquities,
   healed by his stripes."
We ponder how much self-giving could heal our lives,
  and we cannot do better than to rest ourselves
    in that awesome mystery.
    All the while we occupy the killing fields . . .
    Those fields always filled
      with Amalekites,
      their Amalekites,
      our Amalekites,
      always Amalekites to be cleansed.
And we imagine, as do they
  that somehow the killing matches our noblest,
        most pious convictions.
You are the one who has spared,
   who has pitied,
   who has drawn the violence short in order to save.
Hold your church all this week
  to the unbearable mystery of your self-giving, and
  to the intolerable burden of our killing.
Move us from the grip of that deathly squeeze,
  move by your innocence,
  move by your weakness,
  move by your passion.
Deliver us from our Amalekite shaped-world
  in the name of the bruised one. Amen.

On reading 1 Samuel 15 while we bomb Serbia / March 30, 1999

Held back

You have texted us yet again
    with this glorious text of homecoming and well-being.
    We have finished with the text of doom and extermination,
    ready to relish your good news of deep wells,
                and safe roads,
                and happy jackals.
    We among your ransomed and redeemed,
    we in gladness and in gratitude.
Just beyond the margin of this text,
    we are your people bottomed in Thursday,
            grieved in Friday,
    our days of doom and failure and death,
    your days of suffering and anguish.
We look past the doom days
    to the Easter page of good news, ready to dance.
In life as in text,
    we would leap beyond where we are to where you promise to be,
      "Ahead of us in Galilee,"
    held back only by the truth of Thursday and Friday
      and by loud crashing weapons,
    held back, waiting, ready to dance, yet held back . . .
           for a little while. Amen.

On reading Isaiah 35 while we bomb Serbia / April 1, 1999

The pivot of hope

This day of dread and betrayal and denial
    causes a pause in our busyness.
    Who would have thought that you would take
        this eighth son of Jesse
        to become the pivot of hope in our ancient memory?
    Who would have thought that you would take
        this uncredentialed
        Galilean rabbi
        to become the pivot of newness in the world?
    Who would have thought that you —
        God of gods and Lord of lords —
        would fasten on such small, innocuous agents
            whom the world scorns
        to turn creation toward your newness?
As we are dazzled,
    give us the freedom to resituate our lives in modest,
        uncredentialed, vulnerable places.
We ask for freedom and courage to move out from our nicely
    arranged patterns of security
    into dangerous places of newness where we fear to go.
Cross us by the cross, that we may be Easter marked. Amen.

On reading 1 Samuel 16:1-13 on Maundy Thursday / April 12, 2001

The terrible silencing we cannot master

Holy God who hovers daily round us in fidelity and compassion,
    this day we are mindful of another, dread-filled hovering,
    that of the power of death before which we stand
        thin and needful.
All our days, we are mindful of the pieces of our lives
    and the parts of your world
    that are on the loose in destructive ways.
We notice that wildness midst our fear and our anger unresolved.
We mark it in a world of brutality and poverty and hunger
    all around us.
We notice all our days.

But on this day of all days,
    that great threat looms so large and powerful.
It is not for nothing
    that we tremble at these three hours of darkness
        and the raging earthquake.
It is not for nothing
    that we have a sense of our helplessness
    before the dread power of death that has broken loose
    and that struts against our interest and even against our will.
Our whole life is not unlike the playground in the village,
    lovely and delightful and filled with squeals unafraid,
    and then we remember the silencing
        of all those squeals in death,
    and we remember the legions of Kristy's
    that are swept away in a riddle too deep for knowing.
Our whole life is like that playground
    and on this dread-filled Friday we pause before
        the terrible silencing we cannot master.

So we come in our helpless candor this day . . .
    remembering, giving thanks, celebrating . . .
    but not for one instant unmindful of dangers too ominous
    and powers too sturdy and threats well beyond us.

We turn eventually from our hurt for children lost.
We turn finally from all our unresolved losses
    to the cosmic grief at the loss of Jesus.
We recall and relive that wrenching Friday
    when the hurt cut to your heart.
We see in that terrible hurt, our losses
    and your full embrace of loss and defeat.

We dare pray while the darkness descends
    and the earthquake trembles,
    we dare pray for eyes to see fully
        and mouths to speak fully the power of death all around,
    we dare pray for a capacity to notice unflinching
        that in our happy playgrounds other children die,
            and grow silent,
    we pray more for your notice and your promise
        and your healing.

Our only urging on Friday is that you live this as we must
    impacted but not destroyed,
    dimmed but not quenched.
For your great staying power
    and your promise of newness we praise you.
It is in your power
    and your promise that we take our stand this day.
We dare trust that Friday is never the last day,
    so we watch for the new day of life.
Hear our prayer and be your full self toward us.
Amen.

Good Friday / 1991

Not the kingdom of death

Christ is risen!
We give thanks for the gift of Easter
    that runs beyond our explanations,
        beyond our categories of reason,
    even more, beyond the sinking sense of our own lives.
We know about the powers of death,
        powers that persist among us,
        powers that drive us from you, and
                from our neighbor, and
                from our best selves.
We know about the powers of fear and greed and anxiety,
          and brutality and certitude.
        powers before which we are helpless.
And then you . . . you at dawn, unquenched,
        you in the darkness,
        you on Saturday,
        you who breaks the world to joy.
Yours is the kingdom . . . not the kingdom of death,
Yours is the power . . . not the power of death,
Yours is the glory . . . not the glory of death.
    Yours . . . You . . . and we give thanks
        for the newness beyond our achieving.
Amen.

Easter Tuesday / April 25, 2000

We are baffled

Christ is Risen
He is risen indeed!
We are baffled by the very Easter claim we voice.
>Your new life fits none of our categories.
>We wonder and stew and argue,
>and add clarifying adjectives like "spiritual" and "physical."
But we remain baffled, seeking clarity and explanation,
>we who are prosperous, and full and safe and tenured.
We are baffled and want explanations.

But there are those not baffled, but stunned by the news,
>stunned while at minimum wage jobs;
>stunned while the body wastes in cancer;
>stunned while the fabric of life rots away in fatigue and despair;
>stunned while unprosperous and unfull
>>and unsafe and untenured . . .
Waiting only for you in your Easter outfit,
waiting for you to say, "Fear not, it is I."
Deliver us from our bafflement and our many explanations.
Push us over into stunned need and show yourself to us lively.
>Easter us in honesty;
>Easter us in fear;
>Easter us in joy,
>>and let us be Eastered. Amen.

Easter Tuesday / April 17, 2001

You who stalk the earth with new life

Christ is Risen . . . He is risen indeed!
You Easter one
    you who stalk the earth with new life,
    you who soar the heavens with fresh governance,
    you who traipse the seas with odd authority,
You life-giver,
    You a strange anomaly among us,
        for everywhere are signs of death:
    . . . Benjamin taken in his youth,
      our tax dollars at work in Serbia,
      endless diagnoses among our friends,
      people made redundant in all our euphemisms
        of "down-sizing,"
      too much money and too little health care,
      your church here and there nearly consumed with anxiety
        for itself.
And yet you appear here and there,
          now and then:
    You say "Fear not," and we are comforted,
    You say "Peace I give you," and we are less restless,
    You say "Go and sin no more,"
        and we glimpse a new innocence,
    you say and we listen,
    you act and we are healed,
    you . . . and us,
    you and life,
    you and newness,
    you for us,
    you with us,
    you,
    you,
    you . . . and we are dazzled in our gratitude. Amen.

After Easter / April 13, 1999

But not held

Christ is Risen!
We watch this Jeremiah mired down in mud, in cistern,
    in fear and hostility
    all around him,
    finally extricated by watching friends who have done your work.
We watch this Jesus, set deep in the grip of death . . . but not held!
    held over night,
        but not held;
    held two nights,
        but not held;
    Because the power of death could not hold him.
We know ourselves to be held,
    over night, for two nights, too long,
    held by fear and anxiety,
    held by grudge and resentment;
    held by doubt and fatigue;
    held by too much stuff,
        by all manner of the forces of death.
Held, powerless . . . but turned toward you.
You in your risenness, make Sundays even for us,
        even among us,
        even here,
        even now,
        no longer held. Amen.

On reading Jeremiah 37–45 on Easter Tuesday / April 25, 2000

Easter us

You God who terrified the waters,
    who crashed your thunder,
    who shook the earth, and
    scared the wits out of chaos.
You God who with strong arm saved your people
    by miracle and wonder and majestic act.
You are the same God to whom we turn,
    we turn in our days of trouble,
        and in our weary nights;
    we look for steadfast love and are dismayed,
    we wait for your promises, but wait in fatigue,
    we ponder your forgetfulness and lack of compassion,
        and we grow silent.
Our lives, addressed to you,
    have this bitter-sweet taste of
        loud-clashing miracles and weak-kneed doubt.
    So we come in our bewilderment and wonderment,
        deeply trusting, almost afraid to trust much,
        passionately insisting, too timid to insist much,
        fervently hoping, exhausted for hoping too much.
Look upon us in our deep need,
    mark the wounds of our brothers and sisters just here,
    notice the turmoil in our lives, and the lives of our families,
    credit the incongruity of the rich and the poor in our very city,
        and the staggering injustices abroad in our land,
    tend to the rage out of control, rage justified by displacement,
        rage gone crazy by absence, silence, and deprivation,
    measure the suffering,
    count the sufferers,
    number the wounds.
You tamer of chaos and mender of all tears in the canvas of creation,
    we ponder your suffering,
        your crown of thorns,
        your garment taken in lottery,
        your mocked life,

and now we throw upon your suffering humiliation,
    the suffering of the world.
You defeater of death, whose power could not hold you,
    come in your Easter,
    come in your sweeping victory,
    come in your glorious new life.
Easter us,
    salve wounds,
    break injustice,
    bring peace,
    guarantee neighbor,
Easter us in joy and strength.
Be our God, be your true self, lord of life,
    massively turn our life toward your life
    and away from our anti-neighbor, anti-self deathliness.
Hear our thankful, grateful, unashamed Hallelujah! Amen.

After Psalm 77 / March 29, 1994

To make things new that never were

We name you wind, power, force, and then,
                imaginatively, "Third Person."
We name you and you blow . . .
        blow hard,
        blow cold,
        blow hot,
        blow strong,
        blow gentle,
        blow new . . .
Blowing the world out of nothing to abundance,
blowing the church out of despair to new life,
blowing little David from shepherd boy to messiah,
blowing to make things new that never were.
        So blow this day, wind,
           blow here and there, power,
           blow even us, force,
Rush us beyond ourselves,
Rush us beyond our hopes,
Rush us beyond our fears, until we enact your newness in the world.
        Come, come spirit. Amen.

On reading 1 Samuel 16:1-13 / April 13, 2000

We wait . . . but not patiently

Blessed are thou, king of the universe!
    We name you king, lord, master, governor
        and by such naming we relieve our deep anxieties
            in confidence at your rule.
        And yet . . . we notice your stunning irrelevance
            to the issues of the day
            that require hands-on attention.
    We name you king and pray daily for your coming kingdom.
        And yet . . . we also notice that you creep over
            into violence and oppressive demand.
    We name you king and loudly proclaim that your messiah
        will come again, come soon, in glory and power.
        And yet . . . all the while, we grow weary
            with the brutal powers of the day.
    We name you king and wait for your show of
        vulnerability and mercy and compassion
        that will "new" the world and heal our common life.
    We name you, and we wait . . . but not patiently.
Blessed art thou, king of the universe! Amen.

On reading 1 Samuel 8 / March 4, 1999

In these very late days

We regularly say:
    "We proclaim the Lord's death until he comes."
In our primitiveness, we do not doubt your coming,
    soon, powerfully, decisively.
In our settledness, your coming is not too urgent or real,
    because we are venously entitled, privileged, protected, gated.
In our rationality, the "until" of your coming makes little sense to us,
    so we mumble and hope no one notices.

In these last days,
In these latter days,
In these final days,
In these very late days,
    We draw closer to your promised "until."
    We draw closer in fear,
            in hope,
            in gladness,
            in dread.

So we do proclaim the Lord's death until he comes,
    until he comes in peace against all our violence;
    until he comes in generosity midst all our parsimony;
    until he comes in food midst all our hunger;
    until he comes in community midst all our alienation.

We are your faithful hopers,
    distracted by despair, but hoping,
    distracted by affluence, but hoping,
    distracted by sophistication, but hoping.

Come soon, come Lord Jesus, come soon
    while we face afresh your death,
    until you come soon and again . . . again and soon. Amen.

On reading Jeremiah 30–31 / October 30, 2001

Index of biblical references